Decodable Takehome Books

Level 2

A Division of The McGraw-Hill Companies

Columbus, Ohio

www.sra4kids.com

SRA/McGraw-Hill

A Division of The **McGraw-Hill** *Companies*

2005 Imprint

Printed in the United States of America.

Send all inquiries to:
SRA/McGraw-Hill
8787 Orion Place
Columbus, OH 43240-4027

ISBN 0-07-572386-7
11 12 13 14 15 16 17 18 19 20 QPD 06 05 04

Table of Contents

Level 2 Core Books

About the Decodable Takehome Books

The *SRA Open Court Reading Decodable Books* allow your students to apply their knowledge of phonic elements to read simple, engaging texts. Each story supports instruction in a new phonic element and incorporates elements and words that have been learned earlier.

The students can fold and staple the pages of each *Decodable Takehome Book* to make books of their own to keep and read. We suggest that you keep extra sets of the stories in your classroom for the children to reread.

How to make a Decodable Takehome Book

1. Tear out the pages you need.

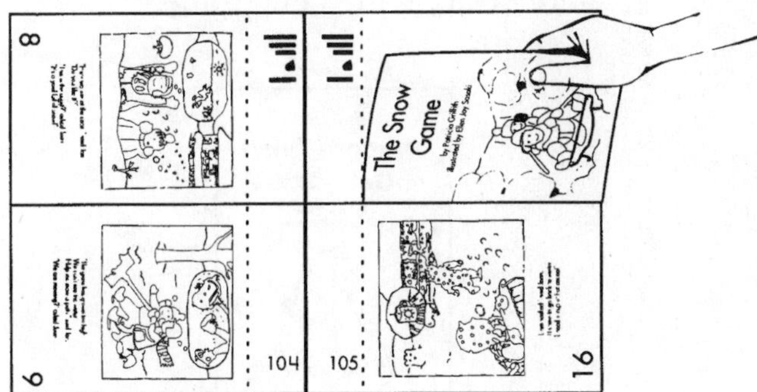

2. For 16-page stories, place pages 8 and 9, 6 and 11, 4 and 13, and 2 and 15 faceup.

or

2. For 8-page stories, place pages 4 and 5, and pages 2 and 7 faceup.

For 16-page book

3. Place the pages on top of each other in this order: pages 8 and 9, pages 6 and 11, pages 4 and 13, and pages 2 and 15.

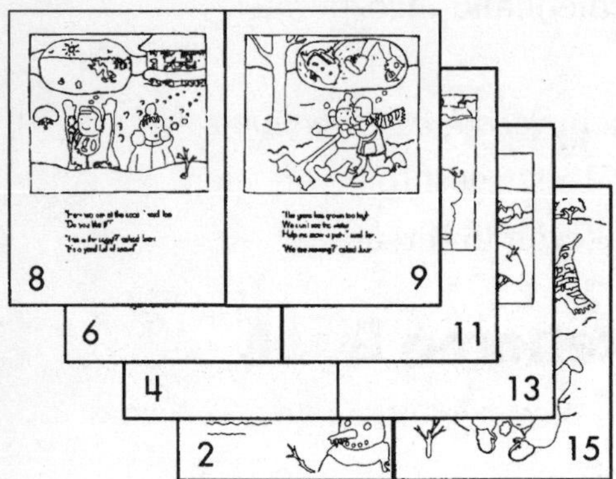

4. Fold along the center line.

5. Check to make sure the pages are in order.

6. Staple the pages along the fold.

For 8-page book

3. Place pages 4 and 5 on top of pages 2 and 7.

4. Fold along the center line.

5. Check to make sure the pages are in order.

6. Staple the pages along the fold.

Just to let you know...

A message from ______________________________

Help your child discover the joy of independent reading with *SRA Open Court Reading*. From time to time your child will bring home his or her very own *Decodable Takehome Books* to share with you. With your help, these stories can give your child important reading practice and a joyful shared reading experience.

You may want to set aside a few minutes every evening to read these stories together. Here are some suggestions you may find helpful:

- Do not expect your child to read each story perfectly, but concentrate on sharing the book together.
- Participate by doing some of the reading.
- Talk about the stories as you read, give lots of encouragement, and watch as your child becomes more fluent throughout the year!

Learning to read takes lots of practice. Sharing these stories is one way that your child can gain that valuable practice. Encourage your child to keep the *Decodable Takehome Books* in a special place. This collection will make a library of books that your child can read and reread. Take the time to listen to your child read from his or her library. Just a few moments of shared reading each day can give your child the confidence needed to excel in reading.

Children who read every day come to think of reading as a pleasant, natural part of life. One way to inspire your child to read is to show that reading is an important part of your life by letting him or her see you reading books, magazines, newspapers, or any other materials. Another good way to show that you value reading is to share a *Decodable Takehome Book* with your child each day.

Successful reading experiences allow children to be proud of their new-found reading ability. Support your child with interest and enthusiasm about reading. You won't regret it!

SRA Open Court Reading

"A frog is from a pond and can swim!" says Max.
"A frog has spots and can hop!" says Ann.
"Ribbit!" says Hip-Hop.

SRA Open Court Reading

Todd's Box

by Chris Meramec
illustrated by Meryl Henderson

Book 1

A Division of The McGraw-Hill Companies
Columbus, Ohio

www.sra4kids.com

SRA/McGraw-Hill

A Division of The ***McGraw-Hill*** *Companies*

Printed in the United States of America.

Send all inquiries to:
SRA/McGraw-Hill
8787 Orion Place
Columbus, OH 43240-4027

"Hip-Hop is not an insect," says Todd. "Hip-Hop is from a pond and can swim. Hip-Hop has spots. Hip-Hop goes ribbit, ribbit, ribbit."

"Is it an insect? Insects hop," says Max.
"Is an insect in the box? Is Hip-Hop an insect?"

"What's in the box?" asks Ann.
"Can we tap on the box?"

"Is it a rope? Is it a big, white rock?" asks Max.

"Here is a little hint," says Todd. "A pet is in the box. It is Hip-Hop."

"Rabbits hop," says Ann. "I bet Hip-Hop is a rabbit. Is a little rabbit in the box?"

"Hip-Hop is not a rabbit," says Todd.

"It's time to turn back," said Pete. "It's getting late. No deer today. Gramps will be sad."

The children hiked back to camp. But what a surprise they had!

"Look who dropped in for lunch!" said Gramps.

Tracks in the Dirt

by Lisa Zimmerman
illustrated by Meryl Henderson

Book 3

A Division of The McGraw-Hill Companies
Columbus, Ohio

www.sra4kids.com

SRA/McGraw-Hill

A Division of The McGraw-Hill Companies

Printed in the United States of America.

Send all inquiries to:
SRA/McGraw-Hill
8787 Orion Place
Columbus, OH 43240-4027

On the trail they came across a black snake, two chipmunks, three puny spiders in a web, a green frog with spots, a smelly skunk, and a slow snail in its shell. But they didn't see a single deer.

The children hiked and hiked, but no deer appeared.

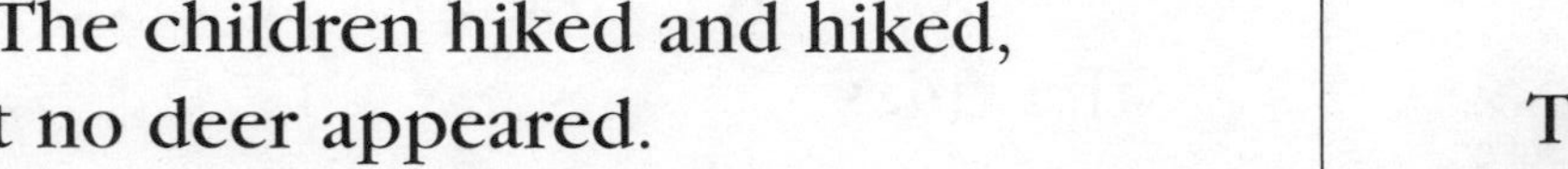

Pete and Lee were camping with Gramps. They spied some tracks in the dirt.

"Look! Deer tracks," said Lee. "Let's see where they go. May we follow them, Gramps?"

"Don't hike too far," said Gramps. "You'll be late for lunch."

Pete and Lee grabbed the horn to signal Gramps and a full canteen to use in case they were thirsty.

"Don't fret, Gramps," said Pete. "We know the rules."

Frank also serves the coldest, freshest milk in the mall.

The Bread Shop

by Tess Baker
illustrated by Olivia Cole

Book 4

A Division of The McGraw-Hill Companies
Columbus, Ohio

www.sra4kids.com

SRA/McGraw-Hill

A Division of The ***McGraw-Hill*** *Companies*

Printed in the United States of America.

Send all inquiries to:
SRA/McGraw-Hill
8787 Orion Place
Columbus, OH 43240-4027

Some breads will be spread with butter, jam, or jelly. All of them will be yummy and worth every cent.

Some of his breads will be sweet and fluffy.
Some breads will be small and salty.
Some will be crunchy and filled with nuts.

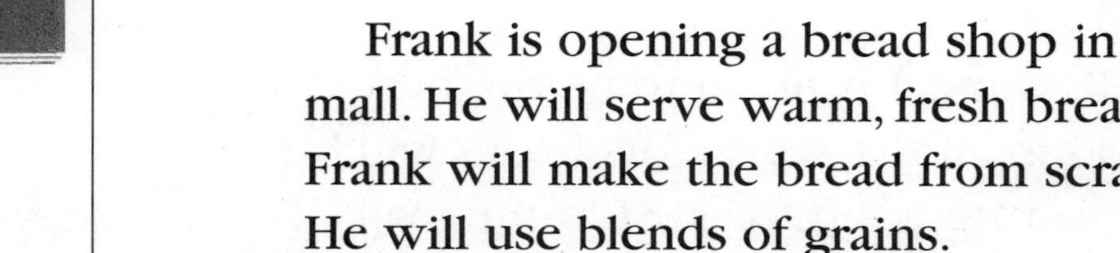

Frank is opening a bread shop in the mall. He will serve warm, fresh bread. Frank will make the bread from scratch. He will use blends of grains.

He wants his bread to be the best bread in all the world. His bread will be the warmest and freshest in the mall.

Best of all, Frank's bread will come in many shapes—a slim stalk, a split loaf, or a striped twist.

Six pups inch up for a hug.
Six pups lick and kiss Phil's chin.
Six pups love and have such fun.

Fun for Pups

by Chris Meramec
illustrated by Deborah Colvin Borgo

Book 5

A Division of The McGraw-Hill Companies
Columbus, Ohio

www.sra4kids.com

SRA/McGraw-Hill

A Division of The McGraw-Hill Companies

Printed in the United States of America.

Send all inquiries to:
SRA/McGraw-Hill
8787 Orion Place
Columbus, OH 43240-4027

Three fast pups tumble and run.

Three black pups wrap up in Phil's rug.

Two little pups pitching and fetching.
Two thin pups dash from a bath.

Two fat pups dumping the trash. Crash! What a wreck!

Mom has six pups to check and catch.

"You sad little turtle," says the girl. She turns Hardtop on his legs. "There, isn't that better?"

Hardtop starts his trip circling past the rock. He still wants the ferns for dinner.

Dinner for Hardtop

by Marian Harrold
illustrated by Meryl Henderson

Book 6

SRA
A Division of The McGraw-Hill Companies
Columbus, Ohio

www.sra4kids.com

SRA/McGraw-Hill
A Division of The McGraw-Hill Companies

Printed in the United States of America.

Send all inquiries to:
SRA/McGraw-Hill
8787 Orion Place
Columbus, OH 43240-4027

"That chirping bird is not far," she says.
The girl spots the bird on the rock.
Then she spots Hardtop.

A little bird zigzags, then lands on the rock. It starts to chirp and sing.

A girl is filling a jar with nuts and ginger.

Hardtop lumbers through the grass. He is hunting for tender ferns. Ferns are a perfect dinner for a turtle. Yum! Yum!

Yes! Some tender ferns are just past the rock. This is just what Hardtop wants.

Hardtop is puzzled. First, he must get past the rock. Perhaps he can circle the rock.

Oh, no! Hardtop flips on his back. He is startled. He wiggles and jiggles his legs, but he does not budge. He is stuck on his back at the edge of the rock.

“That fake snake can keep swimming in the lake,” said Frank. “I can make a different snake.”

The Fake Snake

by Chris Meramec
illustrated by Kersti Frigell

Book 7

SRA
A Division of The McGraw-Hill Companies
Columbus, Ohio

www.sra4kids.com

SRA/McGraw-Hill

A Division of The McGraw-Hill Companies 

Printed in the United States of America.

Send all inquiries to:
SRA/McGraw-Hill
8787 Orion Place
Columbus, OH 43240-4027

"I like the way your fake snake is swimming in the waves," said Gail.

Just then, it started to rain. Frank and Gail ran away and escaped the rain.

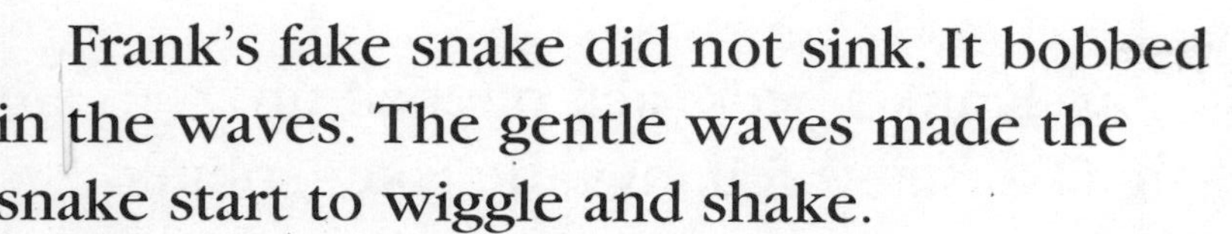

Frank's fake snake did not sink. It bobbed in the waves. The gentle waves made the snake start to wiggle and shake.

Frank was making a fake snake from paper.

"A snake is just a tail and a face," said Frank. "This large snake was fun to make."

Frank had his snake when he went running to the lake. He saw Gail on the trail. Frank waved at Gail and ran to catch up.

But Frank's backpack opened up. The fake snake fell into the lake—plunk!

Crunch. Crunch.

Huge Unit One uses a few mugs for fuel. This time Unit One has energy… and peace and quiet.

Nancy's Robot Tale

by Dennis Fertig
illustrated by Len Epstein

Book 8

SRA
A Division of The McGraw-Hill Companies
Columbus, Ohio

www.sra4kids.com

SRA/McGraw-Hill

A Division of The McGraw-Hill Companies

Printed in the United States of America.

Send all inquiries to:
SRA/McGraw-Hill
8787 Orion Place
Columbus, OH 43240-4027

Unit One does not like mug music. Unit One and Unit Five argue. But Unit One can quickly stop the music.

Then, Unit Five uses the mugs to make music.

Nancy wrote a robot tale. This big robot's name is Unit One. Unit One is huge. It makes the human look quite puny.

This little robot's name is Unit Five.
Unit Five is Unit One's nephew.

On a hot day, Unit Five can use
a few mugs of ice cubes for fuel.
The ice cubes give Unit Five energy.

Gena reaches up and grabs it.

"She is fantastic!" yells Kenny. "See what I mean, Dad? These Mean Streaks cannot be beat!"

Dean's Team

by Marian Harrold
illustrated by Meryl Henderson

Book 9

SRA
A Division of The McGraw-Hill Companies
Columbus, Ohio

www.sra4kids.com

SRA/McGraw-Hill
A Division of The McGraw-Hill Companies

Printed in the United States of America.

Send all inquiries to:
SRA/McGraw-Hill
8787 Orion Place
Columbus, OH 43240-4027

Gena, Kareem, and Kelly are in the field. The pitch speeds past Pete.

Steve, Jeanie, and Becky play the three bases.

Pete plays between second and third.

"A perfect catch! Three cheers for Pete!" yells Kenny.

Kenny and Dad hurried to see Dean play. The Mean Streaks are Dean's team.

"The Mean Streaks are really neat," says Kenny.

Dean is the pitcher, and Dad's niece, Kay, is the catcher.

Dean hurls the pitch.

Jim is the batter. He swings and misses.

"Sweet pitch, Dean!" yells Kenny.

"Mom, those men and women are real heroes," says Joey.

"So are you, Joey," says Mom.

Heroes

by Dennis Fertig
illustrated by Gary Undercuffler

Book 10

SRA
A Division of The McGraw-Hill Companies
Columbus, Ohio

www.sra4kids.com

SRA/McGraw-Hill

A Division of The **McGraw-Hill** *Companies*

Printed in the United States of America.

Send all inquiries to:
SRA/McGraw-Hill
8787 Orion Place
Columbus, OH 43240-4027

Joey sees the firefighters soak the Nolans' home. The water flow stops the fire. The Nolans' home is safe.

The firefighters hurry, hurry, hurry! They slide on the pole. They put on their yellow coats and jump in the fire truck.

Smoke rose high in the sky. Joey rode his bike up the road to see why.

"Oh, no," said Joey. "The Nolans' home is burning, and I know that no one is home."

"Mom, smoke is coming from the Nolans' home," said Joey.

Mom spoke on the phone. "There is a fire at 222 Grove Road. Please hurry!"

“Now this is fair!” said the monkey. “I will take these pieces as a fee for my opinion.”

After gobbling them down, the monkey pounded his gavel and said, “Remember this decision. Case dismissed!”

The Wise Monkey

by Carin Calabrese
illustrated by Kersti Frigell

Book 11

SRA
A Division of The McGraw-Hill Companies
Columbus, Ohio

www.sra4kids.com

SRA/McGraw-Hill

A Division of The McGraw-Hill Companies

Printed in the United States of America.

Send all inquiries to:
SRA/McGraw-Hill
8787 Orion Place
Columbus, OH 43240-4027

"Fair is fair," replied the monkey. "The pieces must be exactly the same size."

And so the monkey kept weighing and nibbling. He nibbled first from one side, and then from the other, over and over again.

Finally, the sides of the scale were perfectly even. The two pieces of cheese were exactly the same size.

"Aha!" said the monkey. "Now this section is bigger." And he took a bite of the second piece of cheese.

"Stop! Stop!" the two cats howled. "Just give us back what is left and we will be happy!"

Two sly cats had stolen a piece of cheese from their master's table together. It was a nice big piece of cheese. But they had an argument on how to divide it. Each cat was afraid that the other might get a bigger piece.

Finally, they asked the judge to help them divide the cheese evenly.

The judge was a very wise monkey. He broke the piece of cheese in two. He placed the pieces on a scale and watched carefully. One side of the scale dipped lower than the other side.

"This piece must be bigger," said the monkey. "That's not even." So the monkey took a bite of the bigger piece of cheese.

But now the opposite side of the scale was lower.

But the crew knew that the Blue Sox were winning. They could see a clue. What super news!

The Blimp Crew

by Dennis Fertig
illustrated by Len Epstein

Book 12

SRA
A Division of The McGraw-Hill Companies
Columbus, Ohio

www.sra4kids.com

SRA/McGraw-Hill
A Division of The McGraw-Hill Companies

Printed in the United States of America.

Send all inquiries to:
SRA/McGraw-Hill
8787 Orion Place
Columbus, OH 43240-4027

The blimp had to return home by noon.

The flutes made beautiful music. The drum went boom. The tuba blew a few bad notes.

On a nice June day, a blimp flew over the game. On the blimp was an ad for Grandma Sue's Special Stew. That's the stew with tuna in it!

The blimp crew could see the game. One team had red caps. The home team had bright blue socks.

The blimp crew could see the band, too.

This made Brownie happy. He smiled and laughed out loud. Now Brownie is a happy clown! The crowd at the show loves him!

SRA Open Court Reading

The Frowning Clown

by Carolyn Crimi
illustrated by Olivia Cole

Book 13

A Division of The McGraw-Hill Companies
Columbus, Ohio

www.sra4kids.com

SRA/McGraw-Hill

A Division of The **McGraw-Hill** *Companies*

Printed in the United States of America.

Send all inquiries to:
SRA/McGraw-Hill
8787 Orion Place
Columbus, OH 43240-4027

Then a little clown gave Brownie a big hug.

"I don't care an ounce if you do feel low and frown," said the little clown. "I am still proud to have you around! You should not pout and feel left out."

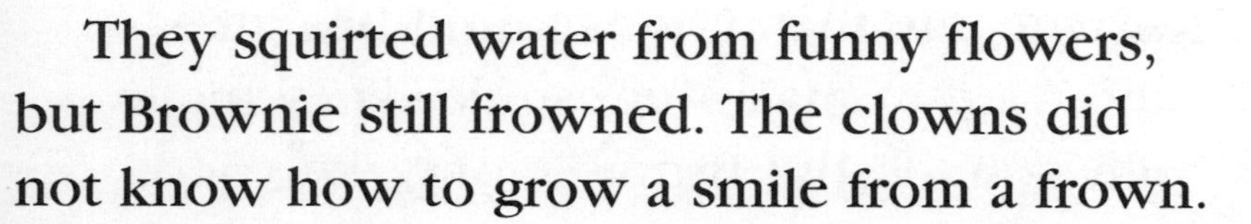

They squirted water from funny flowers, but Brownie still frowned. The clowns did not know how to grow a smile from a frown.

In a brown house, down at the edge of town, lives a short, stout clown. The clown's name is Brownie.

Brownie was sad. He felt left out. He did not laugh or smile like the other clowns. He did not run and bound. All Brownie did was frown.

One day, the clowns found Brownie and tried to make him smile. They made silly sounds, but Brownie only frowned.

"Mmmm! My favorite!" squawked Paul.

SRA Open Court Reading

Claude the Tiger

by Carolyn Crimi
illustrated by Len Epstein

Book 14

A Division of The McGraw-Hill Companies
Columbus, Ohio

www.sra4kids.com

SRA/McGraw-Hill

A Division of The McGraw-Hill Companies

Printed in the United States of America.

Send all inquiries to:
SRA/McGraw-Hill
8787 Orion Place
Columbus, OH 43240-4027

"Now it's time for your lunch, Paul," said Maude. "Here is a plate of dinosaur scales with salted walnut sauce."

"I feed Claude sausages and cauliflower," said Maude. "And he loves to sip buttermilk with a straw."

"What a strange diet for a tiger," thought Paul.

Maude has a pet tiger. Its name is Claude. Claude's paws have sharp claws. But Maude is glad she bought Claude.

"Claude is really tame," said Maude.
"I have taught him some tricks."

Paul watched Claude draw and tumble.
Claude caught every ball in a game of catch.
"Claude must be awfully smart.
What makes him smart, Maude?" asked Paul.

Mack and Nick are glad to nibble, sip, and pick.

They sit back and have their snack and pass a bit to Dodger.

Mack and Nick

by Chessa Danzig-Khan
illustrated by Francisco Rodriguez

Book 15

SRA
A Division of The McGraw-Hill Companies
Columbus, Ohio

SRA Open Court Reading

www.sra4kids.com

SRA/McGraw-Hill

A Division of The **McGraw-Hill** *Companies*

Printed in the United States of America.

Send all inquiries to:
SRA/McGraw-Hill
8787 Orion Place
Columbus, OH 43240-4027

Nick and Mack are glad!
Glad to kick and nudge the stack,
to get the stick,
to have the backpack,
to have the fudge and popcorn snack,
back from the pick-up stick stack.

Mack

An ant named Mack has a black backpack.
His best friend Nick has a pet named Dodger.

Mack is on a pick-up stick.
The stick is in a stack.
Mack uses it like a bridge.

Nick picks a stick and kicks the stack. He kicks and nudges the stack until they get Mack's backpack.

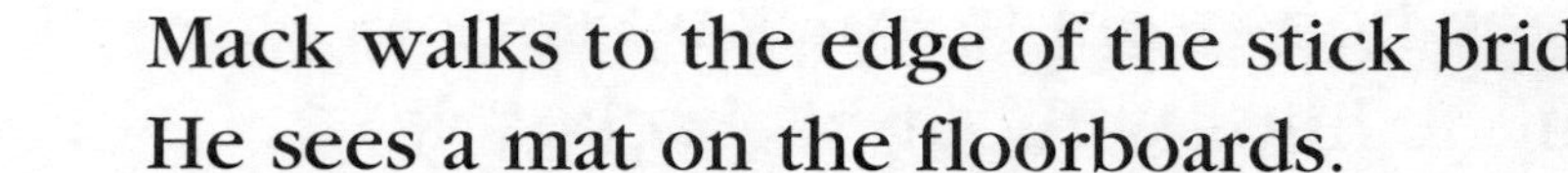

Mack walks to the edge of the stick bridge. He sees a mat on the floorboards.

Mack hops from the pick-up stick,
but he hops without his backpack.

Nick

Mack's friend, Nick, can help Mack with the stick and the backpack and the snack.

Mack must have his snack.
His snack is fudge and popcorn.
His snack is in his backpack.

But his backpack and snack are on the stick, and the stick is in the stack. What can he do?

Help! Help! Help!

"A hot dog is the best lunch!" said Matt.

The Best Lunch

by Karen Herzoff
illustrated by Jack Compton

Book 16

SRA
A Division of The McGraw-Hill Companies
Columbus, Ohio

www.sra4kids.com

SRA/McGraw-Hill

A Division of The **McGraw-Hill** *Companies*

Printed in the United States of America.

Send all inquiries to:
SRA/McGraw-Hill
8787 Orion Place
Columbus, OH 43240-4027

"Not a hot dog with a bun?" asked Mom.

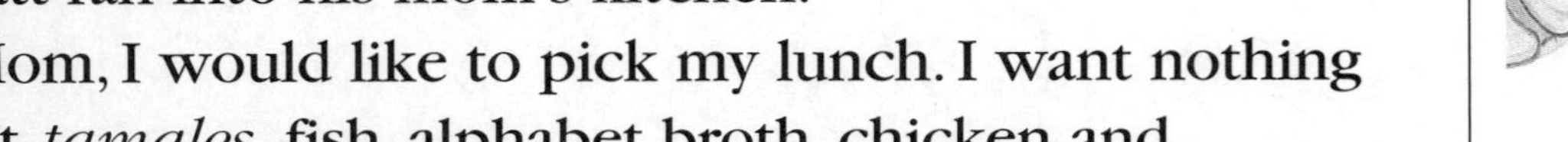

Matt ran into his mom's kitchen.
"Mom, I would like to pick my lunch. I want nothing but *tamales,* fish, alphabet broth, chicken and dumplings, and shrimp."

Chapter 1

Class is out. Matt is thinking of lunch.
"What is the best lunch?" asked Matt.

Matt stopped at Beth's.
"What is that?" asked Matt.

"It's a *tamale*. It's wrapped in a husk," said Beth.

"That must be the best lunch!" said Matt.

Matt wished for shrimp for lunch.

Next Matt went to Elena's.
"What is that?" asked Matt.

"It's shrimp," said Elena.

"That must be the best lunch!" said Matt.

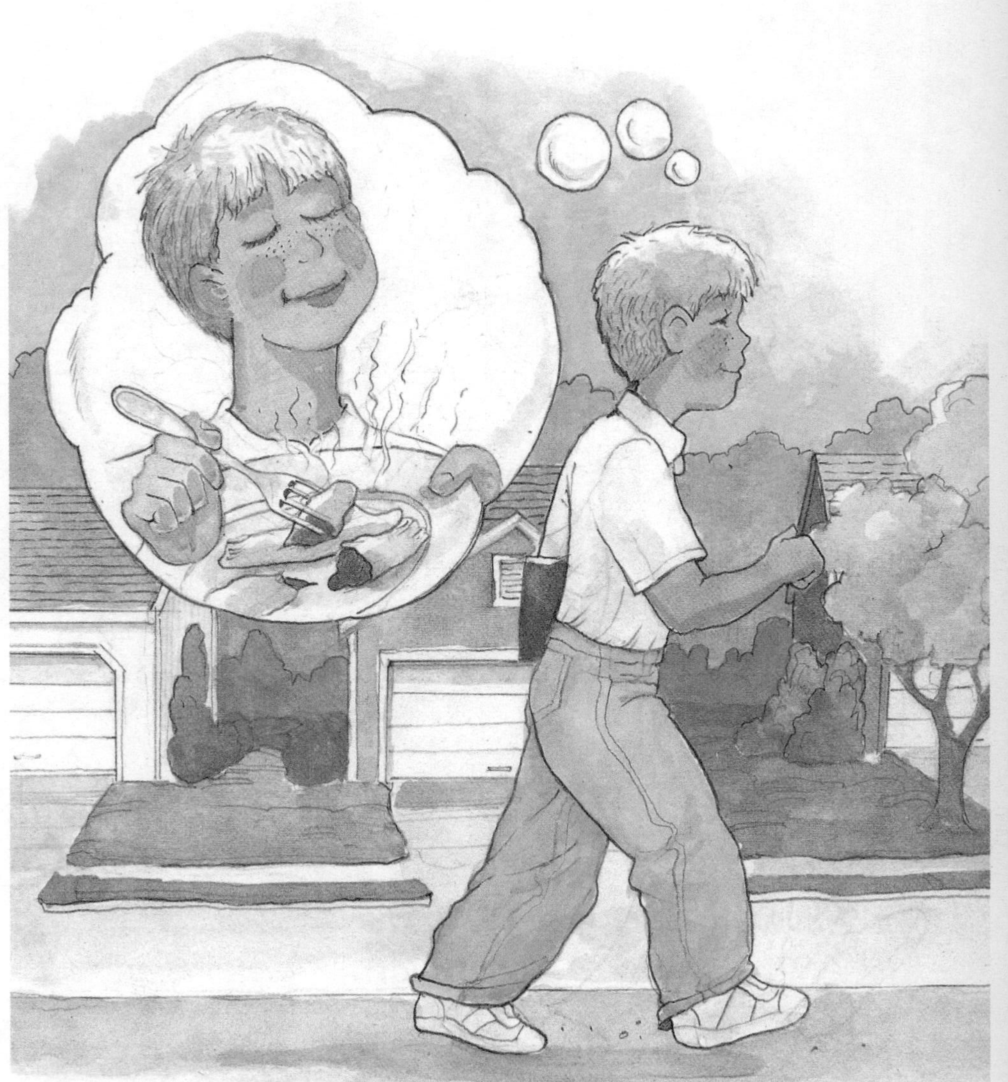

Matt wished for *tamales* for lunch.

Next Matt stopped at Phil's.
"What is that?" asked Matt.

"It's fish in a pan," said Phil.

"That must be the best lunch!" said Matt.

Matt wished for chicken and dumplings for lunch.

Chapter 2

Next Matt stopped to see Mitch.
"What is that?" asked Matt.

"Chicken and dumplings," said Mitch.

"That must be the best lunch!" said Matt.

Matt wished for fish for lunch.

Then Matt stopped at Karen's.
"What is that?" asked Matt.

"It's a pot of alphabet broth," said Karen.

"That must be the best lunch!" said Matt.

Matt wished for a pot of alphabet broth for lunch.

"I got the letter," Jill said. "Can we dance that dance?"

"Yes," said Jack. "Let's dance!"

Jack and Jill snapped and stamped. They turned and clapped.

Then Jack said, "Let's have a snack!" And they had cake, in fact.

At the end of the day, Jack said to Jill:

"I liked all the nice places, but I've had my fill. It's just not the same without you, Jill."

SRA OPEN COURT READING

Jack's Trip

by Kirsten Anderson
illustrated by Dave Fischer

Book 17

A Division of The McGraw-Hill Companies
Columbus, Ohio

www.sra4kids.com

SRA/McGraw-Hill
A Division of The McGraw-Hill Companies

Printed in the United States of America.

Send all inquiries to:
SRA/McGraw-Hill
8787 Orion Place
Columbus, OH 43240-4027

Jack got on the next plane. When it landed, Jack ran fast. He ran up the hill and past the lake. He ran, yelling, "Jill, I'm back!"

Then Jack felt rather sad.

"I miss the pail. And I miss the hill and my lake. I miss my snack with Jill. I liked all the places I visited, but I think I will go back."

Something Different

"Day after day it's the same, same thing," said Jack to Jill. "First we take the pail up the hill to the lake. On the way back, I stumble. You come tumbling after. Then we have a snack, and every day it's cake. Day after day it's the same, same thing. Let's go away."

"I think I'll stay," said Jill. "But *you* go, okay? Just send a letter every day."

Then Jack said, "I need a snack."

He went to a snack place and picked the cake.

"I like this cake," said Jack. "But not as much as the cake I have with Jill."

So Jack went to a place with sand and sun *and* water. He waded. He swam. He sailed. He made sand shapes with a spade and a pail. The sun never failed to blaze.

Jack made his plans.

"What should I take?" he said to himself. "A hat in case of rain. A scarf in case it is cold. And paper and pens (for letters to Jill)."

The plane trip was long. Jack started a letter.

"Dear Jill," it said. "I am on a plane."

(That's as far as he got—then he slept.)

The Best Place

Then Jack went far, far away. He gazed out at lots of sand and lots of sun.

"It *is* different. That's what I came for."

He liked the sun and the sand. With water, it would be perfect.

From Jack

Dear Jill,
Here I am in Spain!
Today I watched the dancers.
They clap and stamp,
and wave their arms.
They snap their fingers with a
click click clack. I will practice
and practice when I get back.
Best wishes,
Jack

Jack got off the plane in London.

He went to a park. He went to a palace. He waited in vain for a glimpse of the prince's face.

A cat named Ben gave him a drink in a thin, pink cup. Jack drained the cup.

"This is nice, but I must go," said Jack. Jack waved his hand and Ben waved his tail.

Jack's next stop was Paris, France. He sat at a table and felt the warm April air. He had lunch with a painter who said he had a nice face.

Jack's next stop had no cars. Jack took a boat from place to place. The sun lit up the water and lit up the docks. Jack stared into the water. He stared so hard he fell in! He was saved by a bunch of ducks. He was wet but did not complain.

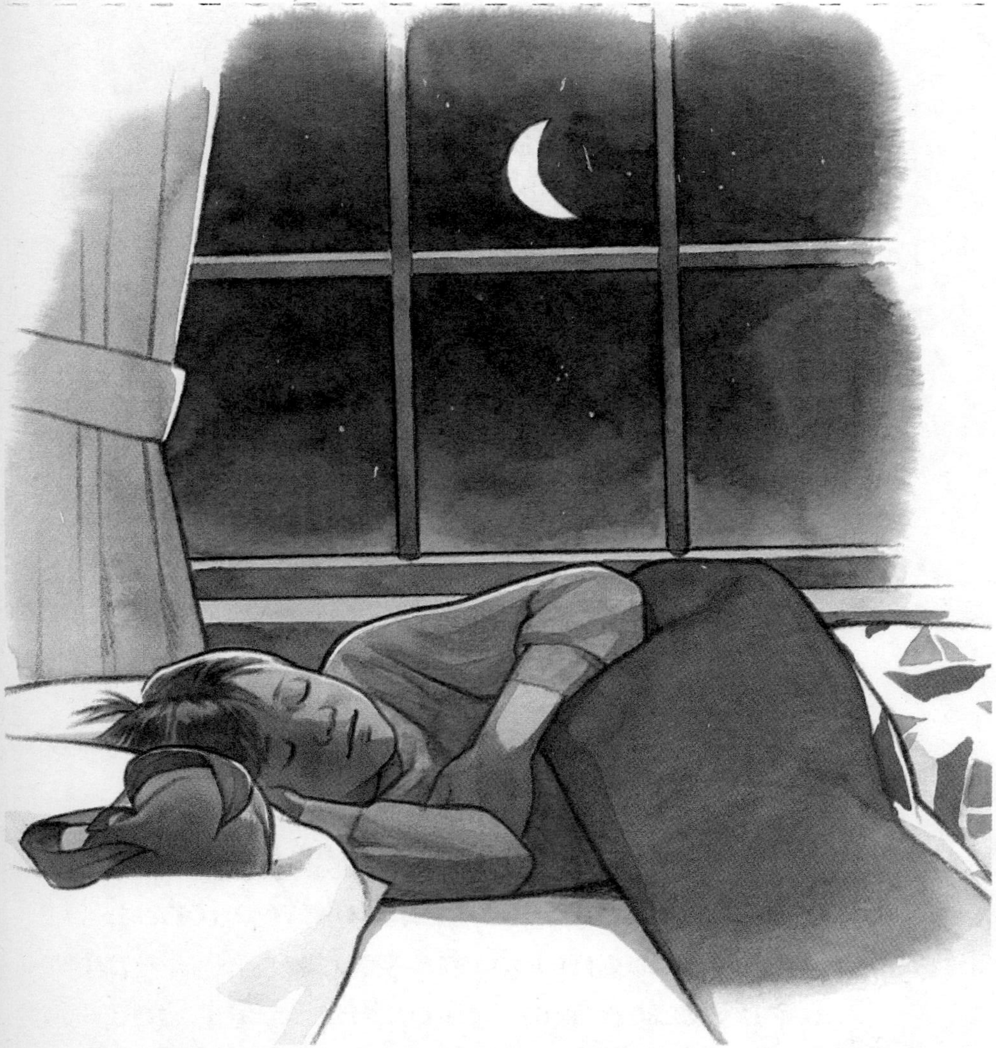

"You are my pal, too," said Peach.
And then they went to sleep.

Beach Peach

by Kirsten Anderson
illustrated by Stephanie Pershing

Book 18

A Division of The McGraw-Hill Companies
Columbus, Ohio

www.sra4kids.com

SRA/McGraw-Hill

A Division of The **McGraw-Hill** *Companies*

Printed in the United States of America.

Send all inquiries to:
SRA/McGraw-Hill
8787 Orion Place
Columbus, OH 43240-4027

Later Peach said to Pete, "Thank you for saving me. What can I do for you?"

"You play catch. You run on the beach. You make things with mud," said Pete. "You are my pal, and that is okay with me."

“You must not leave when I ask you to stay,” said Pete.

“I will not leave,” said Peach. “But I needed a gift for you. It was a pretty, green seashell. But I lost it.”

“That’s okay,” said Pete. “I’m just glad you are safe.”

Peach

“Today is the best day I’ve ever seen!” said Pete. He skipped past a peach tree. Then he stopped.

“Help! Help me, please!”

Who was asking for help?

"I'm here!" said a peach. "I seem to have dropped from the tree. Can you help me?"

Pete looked at the tree. "I'm scared of being up in trees," said Pete.

Peach was not in reach!

"Jump to me!" said Pete.

"Will you catch me?" asked Peach.

"I will catch you!" said Pete. "Believe me."

Peach leaped into the hands of Pete.

Pete saw that Peach was gone.

"Peach! Peach!" yelled Pete. "Where can he be?"

"Here I am! I am on this piece of rock!" said Peach.

"Oh," said the peach sadly. "What will I do?" The peach began to weep.

"Can you play catch? Can you run on the beach? Can you make things with mud?" asked Pete.

"I can!" said the peach.

"Then come with me!" said Pete.

Pete and Peach had lots of fun.
They played catch.
They made heaps of mud shapes.
When it rained, they drew ships at sea.

Peach picked up the seashell.
Then a wave picked up Peach!

Peach went on the sandy beach. He looked at seashells until he saw one he liked. It was a pretty, pale green. It would make the perfect gift for Pete.

Some days they would have a seat under a tree. There they would speak of the sea and the beach. They would hear birds peep and tweet.

Beach

One day, Mom said, "Let's go to the beach!"
Pete and Peach played in the sand.
They swam in the waves.

Then Mom said, "Let's take a rest!"

"Stay on the sheet," Pete said. "It is easy for a wave to sweep you off the beach."

Then Pete went to sleep, but Peach did not. He gazed at the sea.

"I will get Pete a special treat," said Peach to himself.

Not all nights are lit up with sights in the sky.
Some nights are nice with ice cream and pie.
Some nights there's a cat, and some nights there's a ride.
But all nights are fun with your pals by your side.

Night Sights

by Reyna Eisenstack
illustrated by Barbara J. Counseller

Book 19

SRA
A Division of The McGraw-Hill Companies
Columbus, Ohio

www.sra4kids.com

SRA/McGraw-Hill

A Division of The **McGraw-Hill** *Companies*

Printed in the United States of America.

Send all inquiries to:
SRA/McGraw-Hill
8787 Orion Place
Columbus, OH 43240-4027

The night was not like Friday, there were no rides in sight.
No lights in the sky to light up the night.
But there was pie and ice cream and Linus the cat.
A nice kind of night when you put it like that.

So we all ran to Ike's. We got there by nine.
We petted Ike's cat, Linus, while we waited in line.
The night turned out well, the night turned out right,
And I decided to get the Butterscotch Delight!

Night Sights

Friday night, there was an exciting sight!
What a sight, that Friday night!
We ran and ran with all our might
to see the sight on Friday night.

Mom, Mike, Dinah, Simon, and I
went to the field so we could spy…
a place where lights lit up the sky!
Ran so fast, nearly passed it by.

"Mike is right," said Dinah. And Simon agreed.
We looked at each other. We were sad indeed.
Then I said, "Here is what we can do!
We can go to Ike's for pie and ice cream, too!"

No! There were no sights that night, and no rides in sight!
Friday night was the very last night!
"So what do we do?" said Mike to me.
"There are no rides to ride and no sights to see!"

The lights did shine in the night sky.
And we saw rides that we could try.
Dinah and Simon and Mike and I
saw lots of rides high in the sky.

"You can go on that ride," Mom said to me.
We went on the ride, as high as could be.
The ride was exciting. The ride was fun.
Then the ride stopped. And the ride was done.

Mike and Dinah and Simon and I
went with my mom so we could spy...
the place where lights lit up the sky!
We ran so fast. But did we pass it by?

The Next Night

The Friday night sights were such a delight
we decided to go back the very next night!
We ran and ran with all our might
to see the sights the very next night.

At the fair that night, we saw many more sights.

And then it was time to say good night!

The quarter landed. It was tails! Hugo turned around just in time. A huge parade was passing the diner!

"Now you have quite a story!" said Quentin. "The *Tribune* will really like this!"

Hugo was quite amused. "May I quote you?" he asked.

SRA Open Court Reading

Hugo Quinn of the *Daily Tribune*

by Reyna Eisenstack
illustrated by Karen Tafoya

Book 20

SRA
A Division of The McGraw-Hill Companies
Columbus, Ohio

www.sra4kids.com

SRA/McGraw-Hill

A Division of The McGraw-Hill Companies

Printed in the United States of America.

Send all inquiries to:
SRA/McGraw-Hill
8787 Orion Place
Columbus, OH 43240-4027

"Hugo! It really is a parade! And it's quite huge!" screamed Quentin.

Hugo got out a quarter. "If this lands on tails, then I will believe you," said Hugo.

The music got even louder.

“No, not Mrs. Quill,” said Quentin. “There will be a parade here on Cumin Street!”

“I don’t believe it,” muttered Hugo. And then he was quiet. He ate his cucumber salad and cheese sandwich.

Where’s the Parade?

It was a quiet summer day. It was hot and humid. Hugo Quinn had quite a lot to do.

Hugo wrote for the *Daily Tribune* newspaper. He wrote the human interest stories. Hugo's human interest stories were quite fun to read. Hugo liked to amuse.

"There is no parade today," muttered Hugo. "It was just Mrs. Quill on Cue Avenue. She plays her music quite loudly!"

"Why do you look so blue?" asked Quentin.

"I still have no story for today!" said Hugo.

"That is quite sad," said Quentin. "But maybe you can write about the parade!"

Hugo spoke with the public each day. This is the way he came up with his stories. Today a man told Hugo there was music on Cue Avenue. This was quite odd.

Cue Avenue was a quiet avenue. Why did it have music today? Hugo went quickly to Cue Avenue. "What a story for the *Tribune*!" Hugo said to himself.

Hugo went to a diner on Cumin Street. He got cucumber salad and a cheese sandwich. Quentin, the waiter, said to Hugo, "What a humid day!"

"Yes," said Hugo, "I think it may be the most humid day of the summer!"

There's the Parade!

Hugo came to the end of Cue Avenue. He was sad and blue. He had no story for the paper. "Now where will I go?" Hugo asked himself.

He rested for a few moments. Lunch was what he needed. "After I eat, I will be ready to find a story," he said to himself.

There was indeed music on Cue Avenue! The music was quite loud. "It must be a parade!" said Hugo. "This will be quite a story!"

Hugo waited. He waited quite a while. Then he went over to the huge home at the end of the street. The music was coming from there! Was the parade inside the home?

No! It was just Mrs. Quill. The music in her huge home was turned up quite loud. "Do you like my music?" asked Mrs. Quill.

"Yes, Mrs. Quill," said Hugo. "But is there no parade here?"

"A parade on Cue Avenue?" asked Mrs. Quill. "No, not today. And you may quote me!"

"Thank you, Mrs. Quill," said Hugo. "But now I must go."

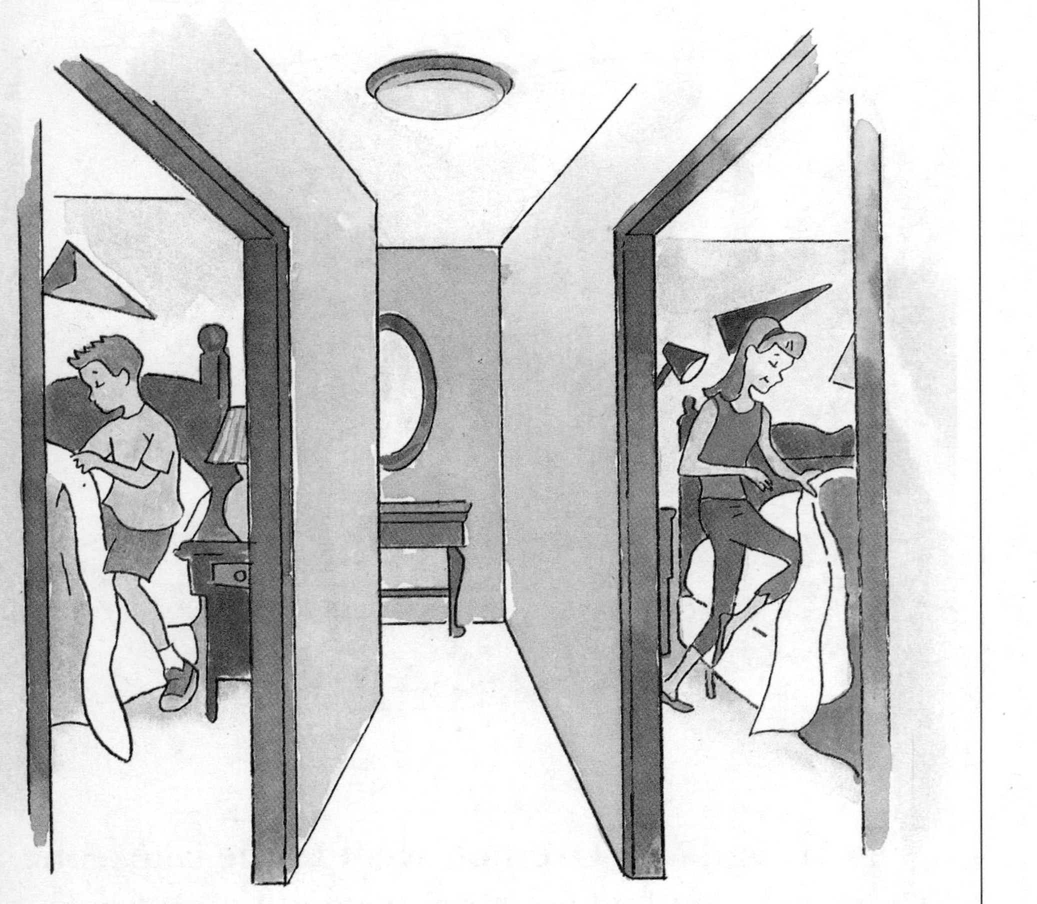

After eating eggs and toast, they put on their clothes and went to bed.

The Overholts

by Dede Mack
illustrated by Francisco Rodriguez

Book 21

SRA
A Division of The McGraw-Hill Companies
Columbus, Ohio

www.sra4kids.com
SRA/McGraw-Hill
A Division of The **McGraw-Hill** *Companies*

Printed in the United States of America.

Send all inquiries to:
SRA/McGraw-Hill
8787 Orion Place
Columbus, OH 43240-4027

So Mr. and Mrs. Overholt went to the lake alone. They each grabbed an oar and rowed their boat until the low sun told them it was time to go. Joe and Joan were waiting at home.

Just then Moe Overholt poked his head out and yelled, "Isn't it a fine day for a boat ride? Will you go rowing with us on the lake?"

"We'd love to," replied Mrs. Lopez quickly, "but this is a work day for us. Don't you and Mrs. Overholt work, too? What will happen if that place of yours is not open—So What?"

"That's how we feel," said Mr. Overholt.

Good Night, Sun

Most folks in Lowell knew the Overholts. They lived in an old stone bungalow on Grove Road, one of Lowell's most charming homes.

Moe Overholt wrote poetry and owned a fabric store named So What. Flo Overholt was devoted to her rose beds. Little Joe Overholt rode a skateboard like a pro and hardly ever groaned about his chores. And Joan Overholt did not mope or scream "Leave me alone" or stay on the phone too long. Overall, the Overholts seemed perfectly—well, normal.

"Those Overholts!" Mrs. Lopez sighed, shaking her head. "Nicest family around, only—"

"I know, dear," said her husband.

"If only I—"

"I know, dear," said her husband.

"But, they're very—"

"You're so right, dear," said her husband.

Mr. and Mrs. Lopez were seeing little José off to school. José waved to them, but they were far more interested in the goings-on at the Overholt's home.

So it might surprise you to know that the Overholts did everything topsy-turvy.

Today, like every day, the Overholt children rose before the alarm went off. They put on their pajamas and bathrobes and marched in to dinner. "Eat more slowly, you'll be late for school," Mrs. Overholt advised.

Those Overholts!

Joe and Joan Overholt left their home together, as they did most days. "Open the door behind you!" Mrs. Overholt yelled from the kitchen.

"Hello, kids! It's so nice to see you!" yelled Mr. Overholt from the driveway.

"You're perfectly right, dear," said Mr. Overholt. He poked his head under the table. "More?" he asked Rover. "More rib roast?"

Ever so slowly, Rover crept out. Then he rolled over and played dead, holding the pose for the whole rest of the day.

"No," said Joan. "I won't."

"That's a good girl," said Mrs. Overholt happily.

"Well, *I* will," said Joe.

"Do as your mom asks," said Mr. Overholt.

"Okay, Dad," Joe said.

Mrs. Overholt ruffled Joe's hair and kissed his forehead.

"That's good," she said. "So, more roast?"

"Do we have any bones?" asked Mr. Overholt. "Or only meat? I *do* hope you haven't thrown the bones to Rover."

"Oh, no!" chuckled Mrs. Overholt. "Rover only gets meat! The bones go to my darling, devoted family. We can thank Rover for getting rid of the meat for us."

She said, "You need to take a nap!"
And so I curled up in her lap.

My Great Day

by Chessa Danzig-Khan
illustrated by Francisco Rodriguez

Book 22

SRA
A Division of The McGraw-Hill Companies
Columbus, Ohio

www.sra4kids.com

SRA/McGraw-Hill

A Division of The McGraw-Hill Companies

Printed in the United States of America.

Send all inquiries to:
SRA/McGraw-Hill
8787 Orion Place
Columbus, OH 43240-4027

Mama reached into a nook.
She then took out a favorite book.
I drifted off as she read on,
until the light was nearly gone.

Mama took a look at me
and sat me down upon her knee.
She gave me something good to eat
and then three acorns, for a treat.

The Trip

I took a ride.
I took a look.

I saw woodlands and a brook.
I saw a sandy, sandy beach.

As I was walking through the door,
the acorns fell out on the floor.
I placed them neatly on a plate.
I said out loud, "My day was GREAT!"

After finishing my snack,
the time had come for going back.
Through brook and woodlands, riding hard,
I pedaled back into the yard.

My only food, a sweet, sweet peach.

I rode my bike; it was a thrill!
I rode my bike down a big hill.
I rode past where a tall tree stood.
I rode so fast; it felt so good.

I stopped to take a little rest.
Then, from a pocket in my vest,
I pulled the very sweet, sweet peach.
I ate it sitting on the beach.

Then, as I pedaled up the hill,
I feared that I might take a spill.
So, at the light I had to stop
and walk my bike up to the top.

I rode to see the sun shine bright.
I rode and rode with all my might.
I rode my bike, and best of all,
I rode to where the acorns fall.

I shook the branch and down they came.
The acorns fell; they fell like rain.
I filled my pocket with a bunch,
and then I headed home for lunch.

Going Home

Again I rode with all my might.
I rode and still the sun shone bright.
I rode so fast; I rode so free.
I rode back past the big old tree.

Badger attacked the drum and ripped its skin off. But—as one may expect—there was not one thing in it. Badger was still hungry, and now the thing was ripped.

> Know what a thing is first.
> Then judge what to do with it.

SRA Open Court Reading

Badger and the Drum

by Marilee McCore
illustrated by Francisco Rodriguez

Book 23

SRA
A Division of The McGraw-Hill Companies
Columbus, Ohio

www.sra4kids.com

SRA/McGraw-Hill

A Division of The **McGraw-Hill** *Companies*

Printed in the United States of America.

Send all inquiries to:
SRA/McGraw-Hill
8787 Orion Place
Columbus, OH 43240-4027

But then Badger's belly went RUMBLE GRUMBLE. Badger decided to have the odd hanging thing as his dinner.

The RAT-TAT-TAT dazzled Badger. He started snapping his fingers and clapping his hands. Then he got up and kicked his legs and twirled in circles. He perked up and, in fact, felt glad.

Hungry Badger

Badger, hungry and grumbling, trudged back to his den. He had trudged since sunup, and now it had started to get dark.

Badger stopped to rest.

When Badger spotted the thing, he thought that it was like an apple. After all, it was hanging in a tree, it had a skin, and it looked yummy.

Badgers are not smart. And there aren't a lot of badgers that know what a drum is.

"This is absurd," blurted Badger.
"I cannot take this drudging and trudging.
I must have fun. I must have entertainment!
I must have dinner in this belly!"

Badger imagined apples and apricots and nuts and figs dangling on all the branches. But that just made him more hungry.

A branch—jerking in the wind—kept on thwacking at the hanging thing, setting off a RAT-TAT-TAT, RAT-TAT-TAT! When the hanging thing hit the tree trunk, it went BAM-BAM!

Then Badger jumped.
RAT-TAT-TAT, BAM-BAM, RAT-TAT-TAT.

Badger darted a look here and there, and then he spotted this thing hanging in a tree.

It was fall, and not much hung on the branches.

Badger started singing. He sang all the songs he knew. Then he sang songs he didn't know at all. But singing made him sad.

And that made him think of his hunger.

The children rested in the shade after the parade.

Margie said, "That was fun. We gave the best parade High Street has ever seen!"

"What can we plan for next Saturday?" asked Irene.

"I think we should have a circus!" said Gilbert.

The High Street Parade

by Karen Herzoff
illustrated by Gary Undercuffler

Book 24

SRA
A Division of The McGraw-Hill Companies
Columbus, Ohio

www.sra4kids.com

SRA/McGraw-Hill

A Division of The McGraw-Hill Companies

Printed in the United States of America.

Send all inquiries to:
SRA/McGraw-Hill
8787 Orion Place
Columbus, OH 43240-4027

People came to the parade and clapped and waved. They yelled and screamed with pride.

Chapter 1

It was Saturday. The kids were playing in the park on High Street.

Margie said, "It's no fun to play on the swings and slide all the time. Let's try to have a parade!"

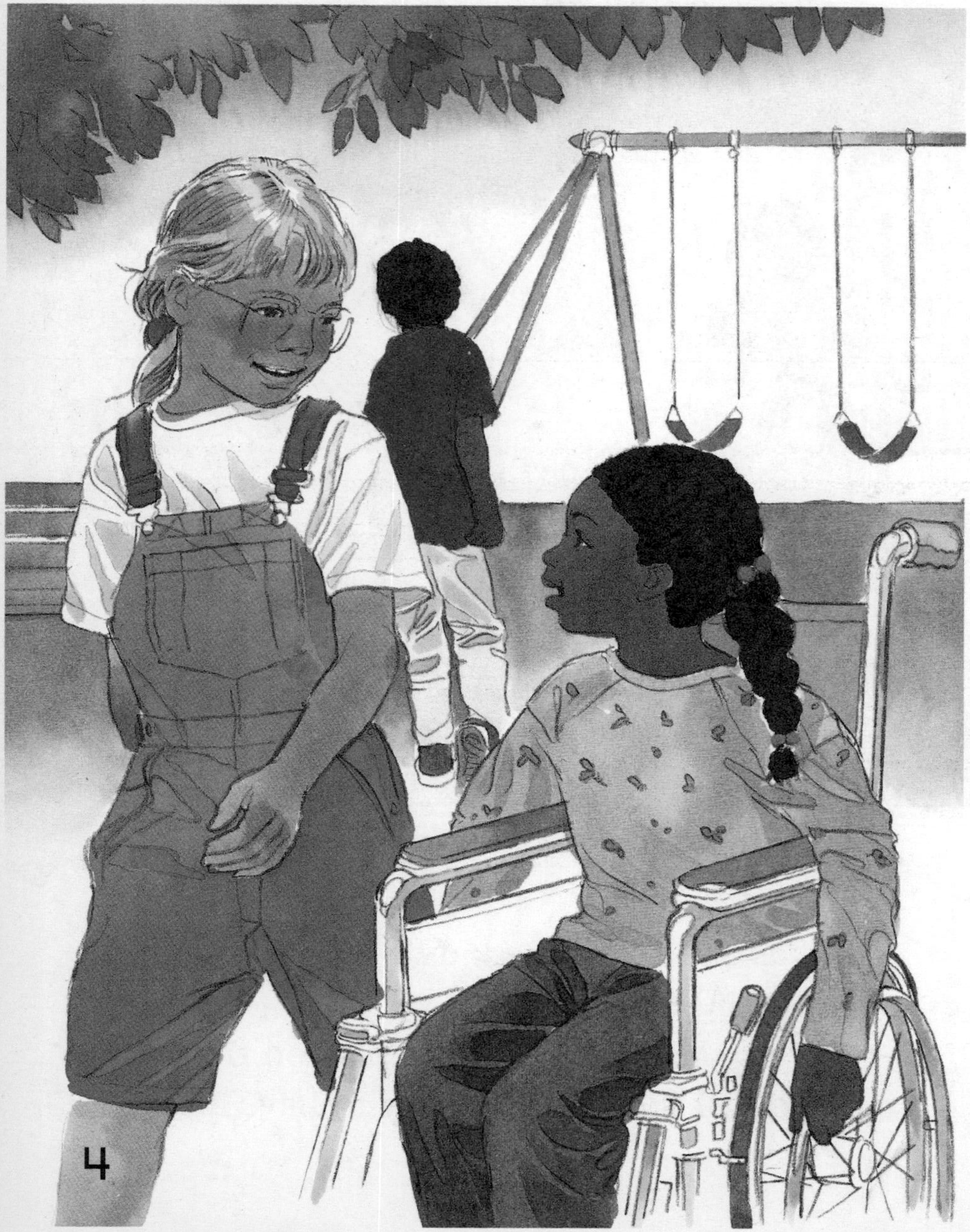

Steve skated. Val and Gail played: Shake, shake! Jingle, jingle! Clang, clang! Tap, tap! They marched up High Street all the way to the park.

Chapter 2

They had a fine parade! Margie raised her cane, stomped, and drummed. Gilbert waved his hat with the bird. Irene danced and wiggled with Ruffle.

"Let's dress up and march to High Street Park!" cried Margie.

Then they raced away to get things for the parade.

Margie got a drum and a large cane. She went stomping and drumming. Then she marched to get Gilbert.

Val had nails to shake in a can. Then she strung bells on her laces. Gail dangled chains and tapped a mop. Shake, shake! Jingle, jingle! Clang, clang! Tap, tap! Val and Gail made a band.

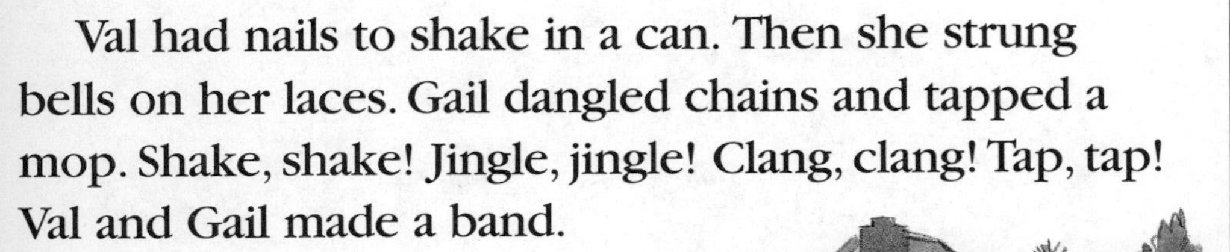

Gilbert had a black cape and a fur top hat. He made a bird with paper and placed it in the hat. They marched to get Irene.

Irene got a lace dress for her cat, Ruffle. Ruffle would dance in a circle and wiggle on her back legs. They marched to get Steve.

Steve had skates that buzzed and a silver helmet. He had a little flashlight to shine when he dodged by. They marched to get Val and Gail.

Dear Arie,
Here is a picture of us dancing the hula. I am so glad you came to Hawaii. Hunny had fun with you, too. Next time, I will visit you in California! Aloha good-bye! Soon it will be Aloha hello again.
Bobbie

Aloha Good-Bye, Aloha Hello

by Ellen Garin
illustrated by Anna Cota Robles

Book 25

SRA
A Division of The McGraw-Hill Companies
Columbus, Ohio

www.sra4kids.com
SRA/McGraw-Hill
A Division of The McGraw-Hill Companies

Printed in the United States of America.

Send all inquiries to:
SRA/McGraw-Hill
8787 Orion Place
Columbus, OH 43240-4027

Dear Arie,
This is what I will put around your neck when you get here next week. It's called a lei (lay). It smells good. I can hardly wait to see you.
Bobbie

Aloha Good-Bye

Dear Arie,
I will never like Hawaii. I miss you too much. I wish I still lived next to you. Mom said it might help me to send pictures and write to you. Please write back.
Bobbie

My Old House

Your House

Dear Arie,

Aloha! (a low ha) Aloha can mean good-bye or hello. Please visit me in Hawaii. Write soon. Aloha good-bye,

Bobbie

Us at beach in California

Dear Arie,

I told Hunny how we play twin sisters, and I told her that our moms are real twins. Sometimes Hunny and I play that we are sisters. Is that ok with you? Write soon.

Bobbie

Dear Arie,
I love swimming in the ocean!
Come play twin sisters, like our
moms, as we did before.
Aloha good-bye,

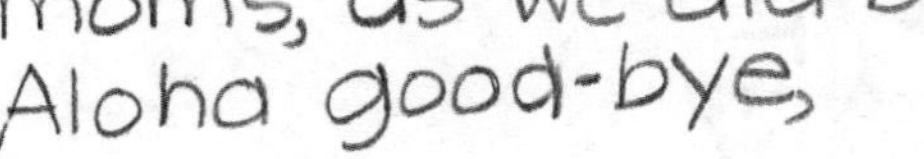

Bobbie

Remember our boat ride?

Dear Arie,

Hunny and I hiked to a dried volcano. Do you want to see a volcano when you visit? Aloha,

Bobbie

Aloha Hello

Dear Arie,
We eat pineapple every day.
When it rains, and the sun is out,
we call the rain pineapple mist.
You can play in pineapple mist.

Bobbie

us in the sprinkler

Dear Arie,
We study Hawaii in school.
Hawaii is in the middle of the big
Pacific Ocean. You will have to fly over
the ocean to visit me. Aloha,

Bobbie

Dear Arie,

Maybe the humpback whales will be visiting Hawaii when you visit. Hump, bump, lump. Remember how we liked to rhyme everything?

Bobbie

Blue
clue
flu

Dear Arie,

I feel silly. Hunny and I take hula lessons. Hula is the dance of Hawaii. Hunny is a girl in my hula class. Hunny likes to rhyme things, too.

Hula-Doola she calls me. When will you visit so I can say Aloha hello?

Bobbie

"Why are you dressed that way, Dad?" asked Brian.

"I'm not Dad. I'm Brian the Fantastic Kid. Everyone knows a kid is the best thing to be!" said Dad.

SRA Open Court Reading

The Best Thing to Be

by Laura Kirsch
illustrated by Len Epstein

Book 26

SRA
A Division of The McGraw-Hill Companies
Columbus, Ohio

www.sra4kids.com

SRA/McGraw-Hill

A Division of The McGraw-Hill Companies

Printed in the United States of America.

Send all inquiries to:
SRA/McGraw-Hill
8787 Orion Place
Columbus, OH 43240-4027

Brian sighed. Nobody saw how brave and loyal he was. Nobody would reward him with gold. How could a kid have some excitement?

"What's going on here?" asked Dad.

"Have no fear! I will save you from the horrible dragon!" said Brian.

"If Muffy is a dragon, who are you?" asked Dad.

"I am Sir David the Dragon Hunter! I must take the treasure from this dragon and return it to the king!"

"I wonder what the king will do with Muffy's dirty old bone," said Dad.

Chapter 1

Brian was restless. He wanted to be like the heroes he read about in his books.

"Being a kid isn't exciting," thought Brian. "I want praise and excitement."

Brian thought and thought. "I will not be Brian anymore," he decided. "I will be Fred the Fearless Firefighter."

Sir David is brave and loyal. He travels the planet. Only Sir David can defeat the horrible, fire-breathing dragon! He can return the stolen treasure to the king! The king will reward him with gold!

Chapter 3

Fred the Fearless Firefighter rushes to rescue victims from burning skyscrapers! He is strong and brave!

"Brian, you're soaking our lunch!" yelled Dad.

"I'm not Brian," said Brian. "I'm Fred the Fearless Firefighter. I will rescue you from this blaze! I am strong and brave!"

"And now you will be hungry," said Dad.

"Astronauts don't get much praise around here," Brian thought. "There must be something else to be."

"I know! I'll be a knight in shining armor. I'll be Sir David the Dragon Hunter!"

"What happened, Brian?" asked Dad.

"I'm not Brian," said Brian. "I'm Al the Awesome Astronaut! I flew fast and far and explored a new planet. I was smart and fearless!"

Dad helped Brian down from the tree. "Welcome back to our planet, Al," Dad chuckled.

"Firefighters don't get much praise around here," thought Brian. "I will have to be someone else."

Again he thought and thought. "I know! I'll be Al the Awesome Astronaut!"

Chapter 2

Al the Awesome Astronaut commands a rocket. He flies faster and farther than any astronaut before him. He discovers new planets and visits them. He is smart and fearless!

It was night. The races were over. Bright stars twinkled in the sky. In a home near Sprat Creek, the smiling twins slept, replaying the races in their dreams. Three ribbons hung on their wooden beds. Each said "First Place."

SRA Open Court Reading

Clare's Secret

by Dennis Burns
illustrated by Kersti Frigell

Book 27

SRA
A Division of The McGraw-Hill Companies
Columbus, Ohio

www.sra4kids.com

SRA/McGraw-Hill

A Division of The **McGraw-Hill** *Companies*

Printed in the United States of America.

Send all inquiries to:
SRA/McGraw-Hill
8787 Orion Place
Columbus, OH 43240-4027

"I am going to switch and enter the long race," said Brad. "Is that agreeable?" Just as Clare began to speak, Brad grinned and skated to the starting line.

"First, I have a surprise for you," said Brad. "Clare, I know you are the faster person in the short race. I have a way we might both win fair and square."

Chapter 1

Clare and her twin brother, Brad, were standing on a small overlook. Below them, Sprat Creek was frozen solid. Across the creek, a sign said:

SPRAT CREEK ICE SKATING RACES

Some skaters and a small, striped tractor were on the creek. The tractor scraped a blanket of snow off the frozen creek.

When they got to Sprat Creek, aimless snowflakes floated in the sky.

Clare said softly, "I have a secret to tell you, Brad."

This was the day of the real races. Clare had to try her best to win the short race. But if she won, Brad might be unhappy or feel foolish.

The skaters were getting set for the races. Some stretched. Some zoomed from place to place. Some twisted and twirled.

Lots of skating fans were standing at the creek.

They had on coats with hoods, extra scarfs, and bright stocking caps. They stomped their feet and clapped their hands in the cold.

Clare's secret was that she was faster than Brad. At practice for the short race, Clare was careful to let Brad take first place. Clare just glided at the end.

This year, Brad and Clare practiced skating every day after school. They skated and skated. Brad and Clare got stronger and faster.

On the overlook, Brad said, "We must get to the creek, Clare." Clare stared at the winter sky. She felt like the sky looked—gloomy and gray.

Clare followed Brad on foot. She wished she could disappear and skip the race. She had a secret, but she was afraid to tell her brother.

Chapter 2

Last year, Brad took the first prize ribbon at the Sprat Creek Ice Skating Races. He was the best skater in the short race.

"So we're still best pals?" asked Roy.

"You bet!" said Max.

"This is the best birthday ever!" said Roy in his loudest voice.

The Worst Birthday Ever

by Lianna McCore
illustrated by Barbara J. Counseller

Book 28

SRA
A Division of The McGraw-Hill Companies
Columbus, Ohio

www.sra4kids.com

SRA/McGraw-Hill

A Division of The McGraw-Hill Companies

Printed in the United States of America.

Send all inquiries to:
SRA/McGraw-Hill
8787 Orion Place
Columbus, OH 43240-4027

"I couldn't come out and play with you because I was making this," said Max proudly as he pointed to the card. "Boy, was it hard! Billy and Andrew helped a little," he added. "I wanted the card to be a surprise. I'm sorry you felt I was trying to spoil your birthday."

"Look at this," Max said.

Max had made the biggest birthday card Roy had ever seen. It was as big as Roy. Roy just stood there, his mouth wide open.

"Wow!" said Roy. "That's really cool!"

What's Up with Max?

Roy woke up early. He was too happy to sleep. Today was his birthday! He smiled, thinking of his party after school. Roy had invited kids from his class. And his best pal Max would be there. Roy and Max did everything together.

When Roy got to his classroom, he went right over to the reading rug to sit next to Max. Max always saved a place for him on the reading rug if he got there first.

"Sorry, Roy, you can't sit here. I'm saving it for Andrew," said Max.

Then a voice that Roy knew shouted, "Happy birthday, pal! Sorry we're late!" There stood Max, grinning from ear to ear. Roy was confused.

"Why didn't you play with me at school today?" Roy asked. "Why did you try to spoil my birthday?"

After a while, Roy began to enjoy himself—a little.

"I'm still having the worst birthday ever," Roy mumbled under his breath.

Roy was upset. Why didn't Max sit with him? Why hadn't he wished him happy birthday?

"I'm having the worst birthday ever," Roy mumbled under his breath.

On the playground after lunch, Roy ran right over to the tire swing. He was first in line. Roy waited for Max to join him. Roy and Max always played on the tire together. They went higher than the other kids.

Pals Forever

The clock struck five, but Roy waited in his room. He didn't feel like coming out. Ever.

One by one the kids he had invited came in. "Happy birthday, Roy!" they shouted. Max was nowhere to be seen.

When Roy got home, he looked at the new toys he had gotten from his mom and dad and from his grandmas and grandpas. What good were they if he had no best pal to share them with? And how could he enjoy his party without his best pal Max? He just knew it would be awful.

Roy waited and waited. No Max. Roy ended up swinging by himself.

"I'm having the worst birthday ever," Roy mumbled under his breath.

After school, Roy waited for Max to join him on the bus. Roy had saved him a seat. Roy knew they would have fun on the bus. It didn't matter that Max had avoided him all day. Now they would be pals again, and at five o'clock his party would start!

But then Roy saw Max's mom drive up. Max and a few other kids loaded into the car. Roy rode home on the school bus by himself.

"I'm having the worst birthday ever," Roy mumbled under his breath.

or perhaps a cow!

A Pig for a Pet

by Marilee Robin Burton
illustrated by Stephanie Pershing

Book 29

SRA
A Division of The McGraw-Hill Companies
Columbus, Ohio

www.sra4kids.com

SRA/McGraw-Hill

A Division of The McGraw-Hill Companies

Printed in the United States of America.

Send all inquiries to:
SRA/McGraw-Hill
8787 Orion Place
Columbus, OH 43240-4027

If you want a pet (at least for now)
try a cat or a dog. . .

Please! Wait until you get a farm!
Then your pet pig will do no harm.
A pig is delightful when you live on a farm!
And you will exclaim, "My pet pig has charm!"

Don't Get a Pig

If you want a pet, don't get a pig.
It's hard to hug a pet so big.

A dog is a better pet for you.
A dog is playful, loyal, and true.
A dog is your friend. She can run and be frisky.
But a pig for a pet is a little bit risky.

You will not enjoy a pig for a pet.
At least not now. At least not yet.

You can pet a cat on her soft head.
It can even sleep right in your bed.
A pig for a pet will destroy that bed!
He will shatter the frame and drip slop on the spread.

A pig will spoil your outdoor fun.
He will not jump. He will not run.

Can you imagine a pig at the park?
The pets at the park all meow or bark!

Get a Cat or Dog!

Or get a furry and cute little cat!
No pet friend is cuter than that!
A cat is coy, dainty, and sweet.
A cat tiptoes lightly on soft, little feet.

Don't get a pig if you want a pet.
A pig as a pet is not a good bet.
Don't get a pig! Instead get a dog.
Or else get a bird, a fish, or a frog.

Your pet will oink. He will grunt and squeal.
Kids will point and ask, "What's the deal?"
You will say, "This pig is my pet."
Their dogs will growl. Their cats will fret.

A pig as your pet will bring trouble to you.
You will ask your friends, "What should I do?"

He will slosh in mud. He will oink a lot.
You will wonder, "What kind of pet have I got?"

Cows moo. What? Who? A cool, morning breeze blows.

I will see you at the alphabet zoo!

SRA Open Court Reading

Alphabet Zoo

by Daryl Edelman
illustrated by J.C. Delano

Book 30

A Division of The McGraw-Hill Companies
Columbus, Ohio

www.sra4kids.com

SRA/McGraw-Hill
A Division of The **McGraw-Hill** Companies

Printed in the United States of America.

Send all inquiries to:
SRA/McGraw-Hill
8787 Orion Place
Columbus, OH 43240-4027

"Wake up, Ray!" Mom shouts.

I hear a *z* zoom by, but it's just a buzzing fly. I wake up and say, "I'm just in my bed!"

"Won't you wake up?" X asks.
"No, I want to stay and sleep," I say.
"Go away," Y replies.
I shut my eyes very tightly.

A, B, C

"I love you," Mom smiles as she tucks me in bed. "Tomorrow we go to the zoo, just you and me."

I wonder what we will see and do when we go to the zoo.

Oh, no! Blooms boom! *P*s explode! *Why* zooms by on a broom.

X, Y, Z

I stare at a bear sitting in a *c* by the sea. The bear is eating an eclair. That bear should share!

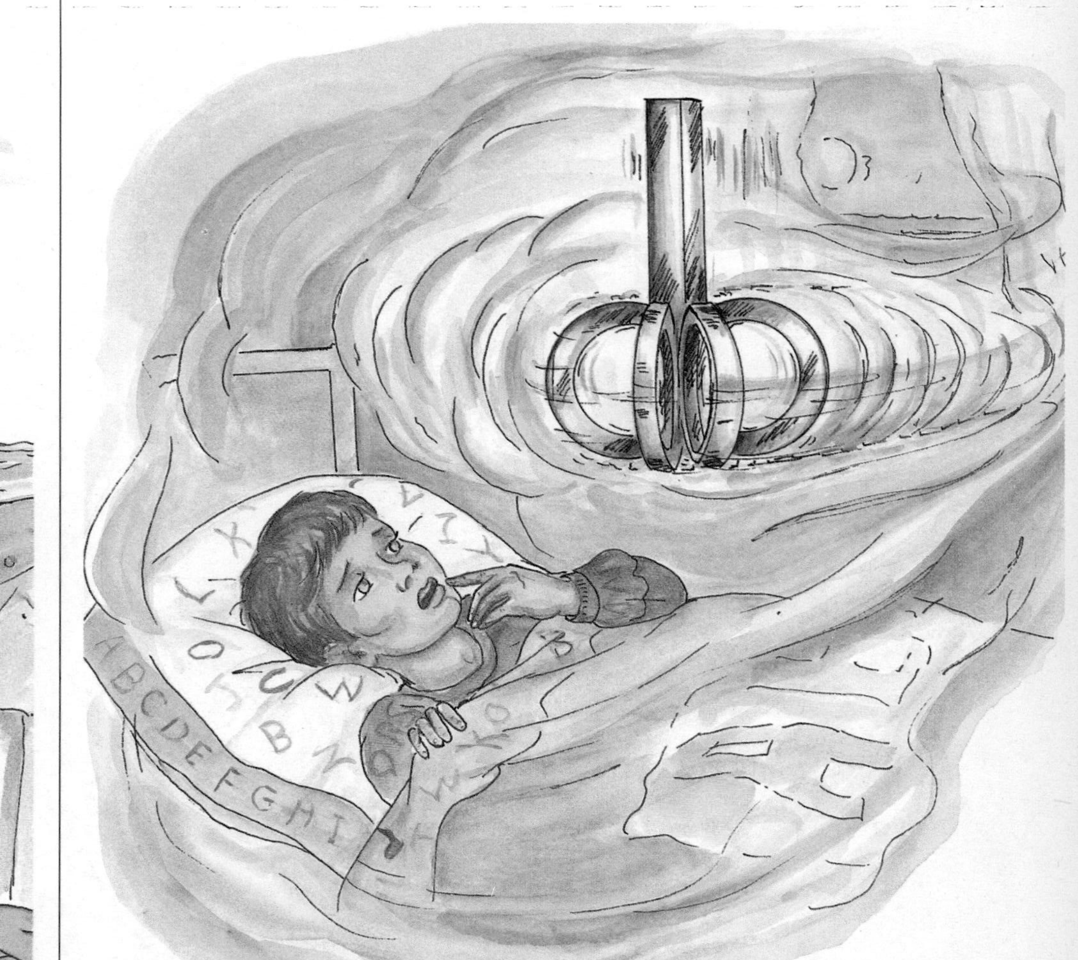

I must be asleep! This must be a dream! I see a *b!*
Not a bee! The letter *b!*
I hear a *b* buzz! How can this be?
I just saw a *b*! Or was it a *d?*

I see *g*s hanging on trees. It's strange to see swinging *g*s in a gusting August breeze!

I hear a short sound ask a long one, "What happens when two vowels go walking?"

The long sound laughs and sings along, "The first one does the talking!"

Sometimes letters like to think. An *m* and I watch a stone sink. A *w* waves in the water and winks.

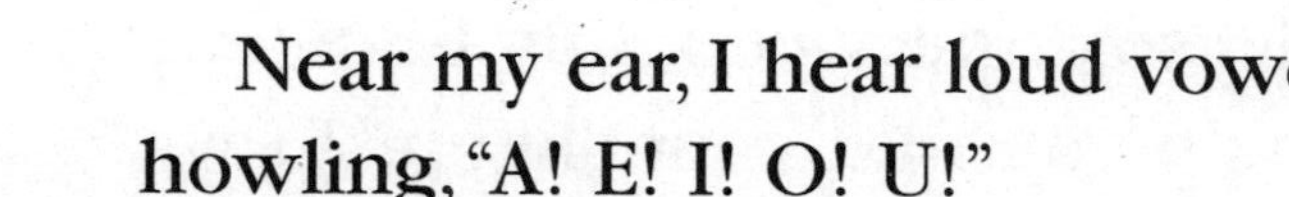

Near my ear, I hear loud vowels howling, "A! E! I! O! U!"

From nowhere, L leaps over Little Bo Peep.

"Please don't weep, silly Bo Peep. I will help you find your sheep," I say.

Letters are free in my alphabet zoo. They sound as they please and do as they do.

As for the dragon, he became a welcome visitor in the town. And as for Mee-Ling, she had the best birthday party ever.

And once every year after that, on her birthday, her friends and family told the story of the brave girl Mee-Ling and the dragon, who together saved the town.

SRA Open Court Reading

Mee-Ling and the Dragon

by Jessica Slote
illustrated by Stephanie Pershing

Book 31

SRA
A Division of The McGraw-Hill Companies
Columbus, Ohio

www.sra4kids.com
SRA/McGraw-Hill
A Division of The **McGraw-Hill** Companies

Printed in the United States of America.

Send all inquiries to:
SRA/McGraw-Hill
8787 Orion Place
Columbus, OH 43240-4027

Forever after, the river flowed down the mountain and through the town. The crops had water to grow. The town was never poor again.

Mee-Ling got up on the dragon's back, and the dragon began making his way down the mountain. Behind him, his long, blue tail cut a path through the dry, rocky ground.

And as the dragon and Mee-Ling walked down the mountain, a cool and deep blue river began to flow after them. The dragon and Mee-Ling drifted on it into the town.

A Dry, Dry Land

Once upon a time, in a land far away, there lived a girl named Mee-Ling. She lived with her mother and her father, who were very poor. Indeed, the whole town was very poor. It had not rained in a long time. The land was dry. The crops drooped in the dry, dry soil.

And that was not all. The town lived in fear of a huge dragon who lived at the top of the mountain. The dragon breathed smoky flames and made fearful sounds. Mothers and fathers told their children, "Never go near the dragon!"

The dragon stopped roaring.

"Never before in all my life has anyone dared to speak to me," he said. "You are indeed a brave child, and a kind one, too! Get up on my back, Mee-Ling, and we shall go to your party together."

At the Top

The rocks and trees shook with the dragon's song, and from his throat came dry, hot dust.

"Alone I live. Who dares come near?
Who can break this curse of fear?"

Mee-Ling was very scared, and she was about to run down the mountain, like all the other times. Then, the fear was replaced with another feeling. She began to feel pity for the lonely dragon. So, she gathered all the courage she could and spoke in the bravest voice she could. "You are indeed a fearful beast. But I have come to invite you to my party," she said.

Now, one day, when Mee-Ling's birthday was drawing near, her mother and father said to her, "Poor as we are, we wish you to have a fine, big party. You may ask anyone you please."

Mee-Ling said, "I'll ask all my family and friends, and I will ask the dragon, too!" And she ran out of the house and started up the mountain.

"Come back, foolish girl!" her mother hollered. "The dragon will eat you!"

"Yes, I wish to ask the dragon to my party," Mee-Ling said, and she started up the mountain.

Her parents called her back. Her friends begged her, "Go no farther!"

But on Mee-Ling went, until she reached the top of the mountain.

Now it was Mee-Ling's birthday, and all was ready for her party.

"Poor as we are, your friends and family have a few small gifts for you on this day. A little rice from the dry soil, a few seeds from the dry trees. Is there anything else you wish for your birthday?" Mee-Ling's mother asked.

But Mee-Ling did not care. She went part way up the mountain. She could hear the dragon bellowing a fearful song.

"Alone I live, alone I roar!
I am a dragon evermore!"

Mee-Ling ran back down to her house in fear.

"I hope you have learned your lesson," said her father.

The next day, Mee-Ling's mother said, "Your birthday list is almost complete. Is there anyone else you wish to add?"

"I wish to add the dragon," said Mee-Ling, and she started up the mountain.

"Come back, silly girl!" hollered her father. "The dragon will knock you over with his thumping, bumping tail!"

But Mee-Ling did not care. Again she went up the mountain. This time she went farther, until she could see the huge dragon as he bellowed his song.

"Alone I live, alone I cry.
Friendless and sad until I die."

Red-hot stones shot from the dragon's mouth. Mee-Ling turned and ran back home.

"I hope you've learned your lesson," said her mother.

Did you know…that the word *yo-yo* means "come-come" or "return" in the Philippines? Kids in the Philippines have played with yo-yos for years, but yo-yos didn't come to the United States until the 1920s. By the 1940s yo-yo experts went from town to town teaching kids how to do tricks. Sleeper, Lindy Loop, and Whirlybird are just a few of the countless yo-yo tricks.

SRA Open Court Reading

Did You Know?

by Yve Knick
illustrated by Francisco Rodriguez

Book 32

A Division of The McGraw-Hill Companies
Columbus, Ohio

www.sra4kids.com

SRA/McGraw-Hill

A Division of The **McGraw-Hill** *Companies*

Printed in the United States of America.

Send all inquiries to:
SRA/McGraw-Hill
8787 Orion Place
Columbus, OH 43240-4027

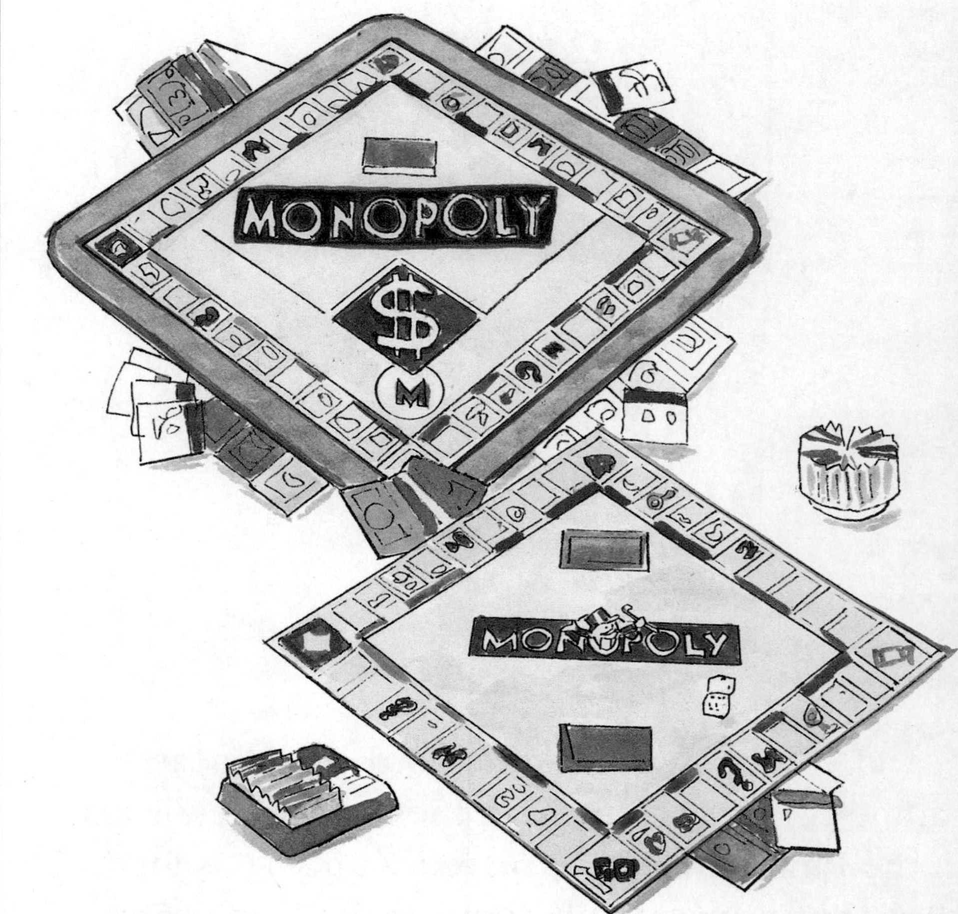

Monopoly was invented in 1932 by a man named Charles Darrow. He used the names of streets in Atlantic City, New Jersey. The first game was made on a plastic tablecloth.

Did you know…that in 1975, printing presses for Monopoly games printed more money than the United States government? The game's presses printed $40,000,000,000 in fake bills. The United States' printing presses made $22,000,000,000 in real bills that year.

Sports

There are lots of different sports and games. Did you ever think about how they started?

Did you know…that a teacher named James Naismith invented basketball in the late 1800s? The first game was played with a soccer ball and round peach baskets. When a player made a goal, someone had to go up a ladder to get the ball out of the basket. When the ball bounced into the crowd, it was out of bounds. The first player to get to it got to throw it back in. Between that and fighting for rebounds, the games could get pretty rowdy.

Over the years, people have used kites for lots of different things. The Wright brothers studied kites to help them figure out how to fly. The first airplane was really more of a box kite than a plane.

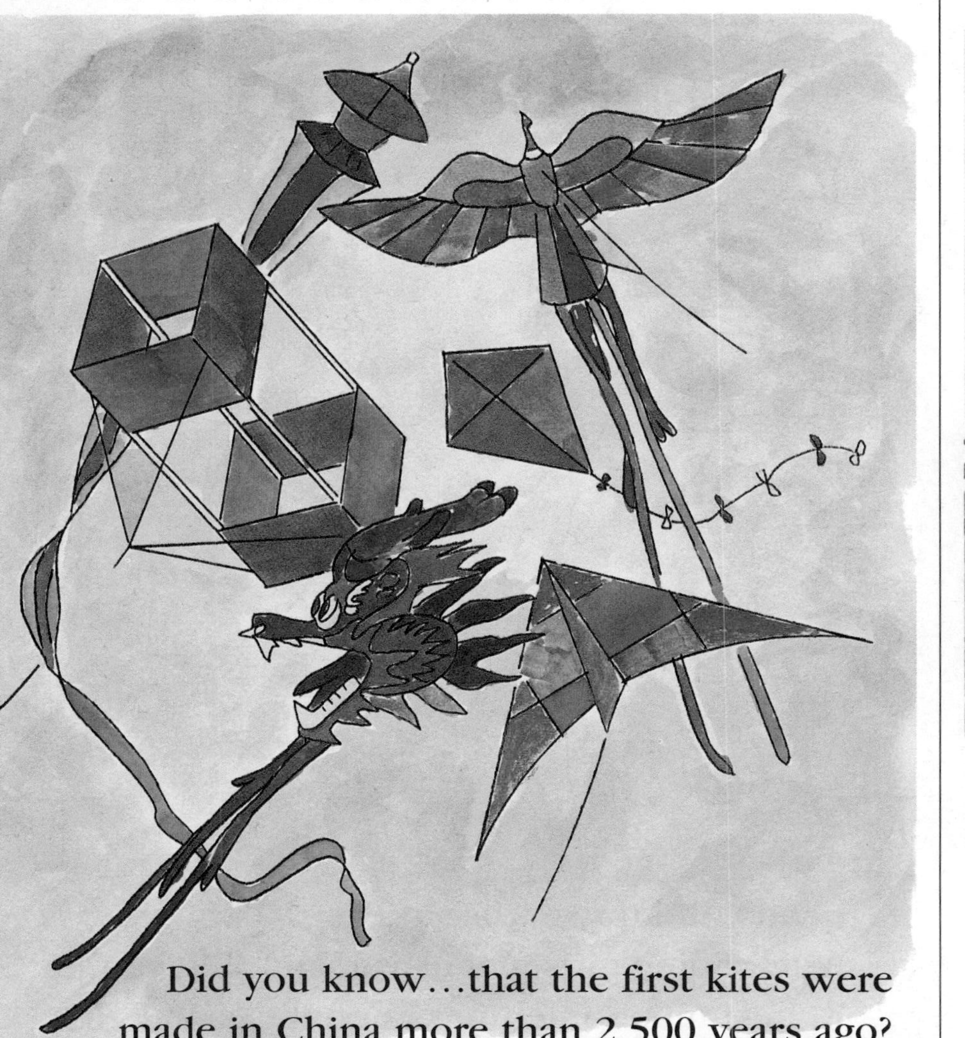

Did you know…that the first kites were made in China more than 2,500 years ago? Historians think these kites were made out of large leaves and twisted vines.

Did you know…that baseball was first named rounders and then town ball? In 1845, men in New York City started the first United States team. They named themselves the Knickerbockers. Players who argued with the umpire were fined twenty-five cents.

Did you know…that ice skating has been around for more than 2,000 years? People in the Netherlands skated to classes and jobs over frozen channels. They made blades out of bones and then tied them on their boots with cow hide.

Did you know…that in Tonga, only girls juggle? Some girls juggle as many as seven limes or chestnuts. Sometimes in contests, the girls juggle so well and the contest lasts so long that everyone is declared a winner.

Did you know…that the first Frisbee was a pie tin? When the makers found that discs made of plastic flew better, they replaced the tin model. In 1964, the Pro Frisbee came out, and Frisbee became a sport. Do you know how far one kid threw a Frisbee in a contest? More than 440 feet!

There are even Frisbee contests for dogs. They can't throw the discs, but they can catch them—in their mouths.

The first ice-skating club was founded in Scotland in 1742. To be a member, you had to jump over three hats.

At first ice skaters were pretty stiff and dull, but in the 1870s, Jackson Haines changed that. Haines added costumes and music to ice skating. He did fancy steps, spins, and jumps. Now ice skating is not just a way to get from place to place—it's a sport and a fun pastime for people around the globe.

Did you know…that bowling is more than 7,000 years old? Rounded stone balls and pins have been found in graves in Egypt.

Bowling has its own word meanings. Do you know what a blowout is? It's when only one pin is left standing. How about a dodo? That's a bowling ball that is bigger than the allowed size. Have you ever made three strikes in a row? That's known as a turkey!

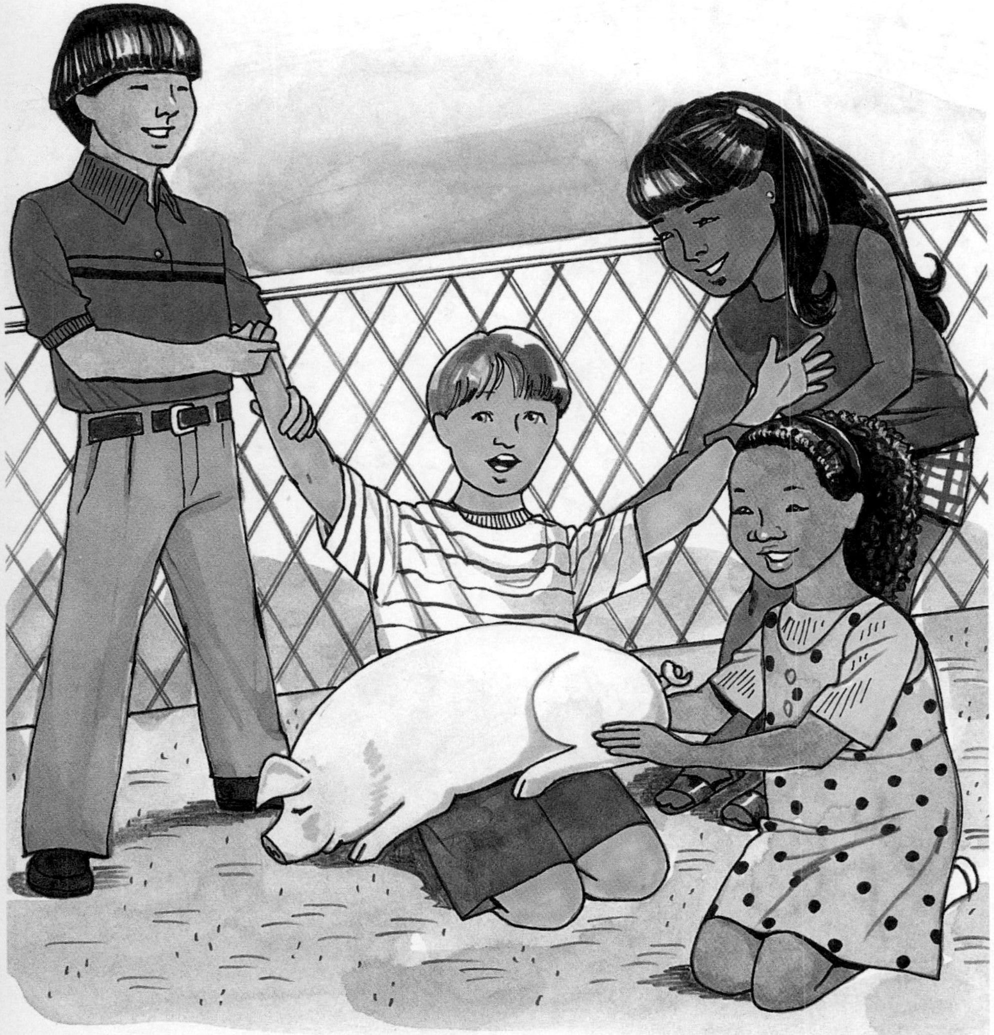

Help!

SRA Open Court Reading

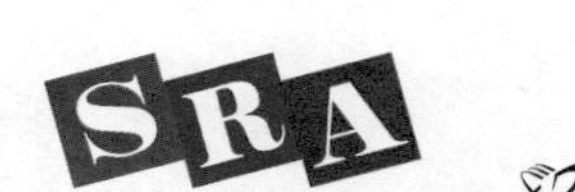

Petting Zoo

by Lisa Trumbauer
illustrated by Anna Cota Robles

Book 33

SRA
A Division of The McGraw-Hill Companies
Columbus, Ohio

www.sra4kids.com

SRA/McGraw-Hill

A Division of The McGraw-Hill Companies

Printed in the United States of America.

Send all inquiries to:
SRA/McGraw-Hill
8787 Orion Place
Columbus, OH 43240-4027

When I got on my knees, Hal sat on my lap.
He had no fear of me. Hal had a nap!

Hal wanted me to pet him, so I petted him.
Hal wanted me to pat him, so I patted him.

SRA OPEN COURT READING

Little Ones

I am Dean. I met Deb! Deb made a peeping sound. Peep, peep, peep.

I am Steve. I met Hal! Hal does not bleat. Sheep and goats bleat. Pigs oink.

When I sat on a rock, Nan sat on my lap.
I could feel her soft coat on my knees.
She bleated because she likes me.

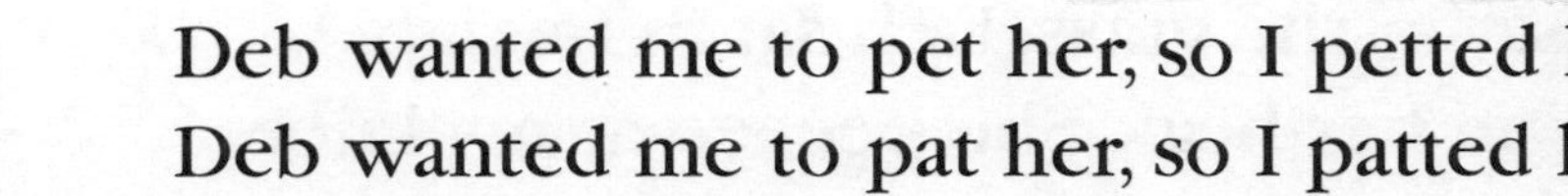

Deb wanted me to pet her, so I petted her.
Deb wanted me to pat her, so I patted her.

When I sat in the grass, Deb sat in my lap.
I could feel her beak. She pecked at my knee.

Nan wanted me to pet her, so I petted her.
Nan wanted me to pat her, so I patted her.

Big Ones

I am Colleen. I met Nan!
Nan bleats just like Ben does.

I am Jean. I met Ben! Ben is a sheep.
When sheep make noise, they bleat.

Ben wanted me to pet him, so I petted him.
Ben wanted me to pat him, so I patted him.

When I sat on a box, Ben sat on my lap.
He bleated because he liked sitting on my lap.

We sit at the table, eating our food,
Hungry and happy and in a good mood.
We had a great day, my dogs and I.
We worked and we played, and watched the planes fly!

A Day at the Paper Plane Factory

by Carolanne Patterson
illustrated by Barbara J. Counseller

Book 34

SRA
A Division of The McGraw-Hill Companies
Columbus, Ohio

SRA Open Court Reading

www.sra4kids.com

SRA/McGraw-Hill

A Division of The **McGraw-Hill** *Companies*

Printed in the United States of America.

Send all inquiries to:
SRA/McGraw-Hill
8787 Orion Place
Columbus, OH 43240-4027

I call them to come, and we're ready to go.
Sam drives by the places we know.
At home we make dinner, all kinds of things.
Bean sprouts, peppers, and donut rings.

The dogs run around, chasing each other.
Spanky trips on his tie and tries to recover.
Sam follows a mouse who runs into his hole.
Spanky leaps in the air and lands in a roll.

At Home

When I wake on Monday morning,
My two dogs bark out a warning.

Spanky says, "Arf!" as I try to sleep.
Sam says, "Woof!" with the clock's beep-beep.

The planes circle, loop, and swirl to the ground.
The dogs try to catch them, those silly hounds.
We test them and check them to see how they fly,
The dogs down below, me up near the sky.

Back in the office, I fold and I crease.
Then it's up to the rooftop with my paper plane fleet.
I sail them off, and they float down below.
The dogs are outside, watching the show.

It's into the kitchen for our morning treat.
They like theirs crunchy. I like mine sweet.
Sam wants a pickle, Spanky a bone.
I spoon out nuts on an ice cream cone.

Time to get dressed and out of the house.
I wear pants with a purple blouse.
Spanky sports a tie and a cute striped hat.
Sam wears glasses. She's funny like that.

I munch on an apple and crunch on a carrot.
Spanky doesn't like ham and decides to wear it.
We eat for a while and finish each scrap.
Then we lie down and have a quick nap.

We work until noontime, and then we have lunch—
Sandwiches, apples, and fruity fruit punch.
We sit outside. The sun shines our way.
Eating again, enjoying this day.

Driving to work is a very big deal.
Spanky is in back, and Sam is at the wheel.
We see lots of friends on the way there—
Maggie the duck and Lazlo the bear.

At Work

We come to the office at the end of a lane—
A funny old place where we make paper planes.
I sit at the desk. I crease and I fold.
I make as many as one box will hold.

I work on the planes. The dogs run around,
Making coffee in the coffeepot and sniffing the ground.
Spanky is dancing and shows me a twirl.
Sam sits at the window, watching a squirrel.

For some, if they cannot have a thing, it must be bad.

Fox went on with his trip.

Fox and the Grapes

an Aesop's tale retold by Tamera Bryant
illustrated by J.C. Delano

Book 35

SRA
A Division of The McGraw-Hill Companies
Columbus, Ohio

www.sra4kids.com

SRA/McGraw-Hill

A Division of The ***McGraw-Hill*** *Companies*

Printed in the United States of America.

Send all inquiries to:
SRA/McGraw-Hill
8787 Orion Place
Columbus, OH 43240-4027

Fox stopped jumping and hopping to shake his fist at the fat, red grapes and grumble, "I am glad I cannot get the grapes. They are sour and bad!"

Fox made one last hop. But he felt sick and very hot.

Sweet Grapes

Fox went on a trip. He ran and ran in soft grass.

The grass got hot. And Fox got hot. Fox wanted a rest. Fox wanted a drink. Fox wanted to cool off. He wanted to curl up and sleep, but he was hungry.

Fox got mad. He stamped and tramped. He grunted and grumbled. He ranted and panted.

Fox stacked bricks to stand on but fell off. Fox huffed and puffed, but he still did not get the fat, red grapes.

Fox came to a glen. He stopped and sniffed. He got a whiff of a sweet smell. He began to feel better.

Fox spotted fat, red grapes on a trellis. Fox licked his lips. "Mmmm. Fat, red grapes. Fat, red grapes are the best. I could fill up on fat, red grapes."

Sour Grapes

Fox got a rock and tossed it up at the fat, red grapes. "I can knock them off," Fox grinned. But Fox did not toss rocks well. He missed and did not get the grapes.

"I can get the grapes," rasped Fox. He picked up a twig and banged the trellis. Wham! Wham! Wham! The trellis trembled, but Fox did not get the grapes.

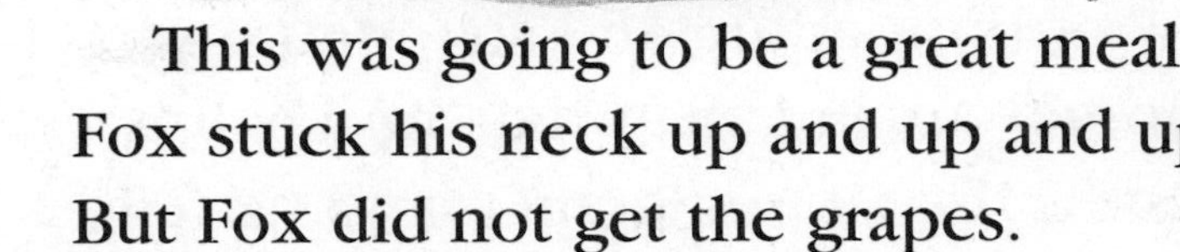

This was going to be a great meal. Fox stuck his neck up and up and up. But Fox did not get the grapes.

Fox hopped up and snapped, and hopped up and snapped. But his lips missed the fat, red grapes, and he fell.

Fox backed up and ran and jumped. He did not get the grapes. He jumped again and again until he was tired. Fox still did not get the grapes.

"Here is the moose, and here is the goose," says Kristen.

"Here is the raccoon," says Fletcher.

"Hooray! We're here—at the zoo!" cheer Kristen and Fletcher. What a vacation!

Toot! Toot!

The Train Trip

by Jo Mintum
illustrated by Betty Leitzman

Book 36

SRA
A Division of The McGraw-Hill Companies
Columbus, Ohio

www.sra4kids.com

SRA/McGraw-Hill

A Division of The McGraw-Hill Companies

Printed in the United States of America.

Send all inquiries to:
SRA/McGraw-Hill
8787 Orion Place
Columbus, OH 43240-4027

"Let's get off the train and check," says Fletcher.

"I see a zebra and an elephant," says Kristen, "but no blue moose."

"I see a giraffe," says Fletcher, "but no gray goose or raccoon."

The train slows to a stop at the edge of the city. The wheels grind and screech. The blue moose jumps off the caboose. The gray goose exits the caboose.

"Last stop," cries Fletcher. "Where is the moose?"

"Where is the goose?" asks Kristen.

Animals on the Loose

Toot! Toot!

"Oh, no! A blue moose is loose in the caboose!" cries Fletcher, the first conductor.

"Loose moose! Loose moose! Time for action!" cries Kristen, the other conductor.

"What can we do with the moose loose in the caboose?" asks Fletcher.

"Capture it," says Kristen.

Toot! Toot! Toot! Toot!

"It is past noon," says Kristen. "Soon we will make the last stop."

"Where's the raccoon?" asks Fletcher.

"I don't know," Kristen says. "Maybe we can see it from the window."

The huge moose stumbles back on the goose. The gray goose honks and chomps the raccoon's toe. The raccoon scrambles and charges out of the caboose.

"A moose cannot take a trip on a train," says Kristen. "The moose must go! The moose needs to be in a pasture."

"Bye-bye, blue moose!" yell Fletcher and Kristen.

"That's a solution," says Kristen.

"Oh, no!" cries Kristen. "A gray goose flew in the caboose."

The Last Stop

Toot! Toot! The train slowly climbs a steep cliff. Chug-a-lug, chug-a-lug. Fletcher glances out the window. Kristen makes a notation.

"That's the raccoon," says Kristen.

Fletcher smiles and shrugs. "I think we must take the moose, the goose, and the raccoon."

"Why?" asks Kristen.

"I believe these three animals will like the last train stop," says Fletcher.

Clip, clop. "Do you think that might be the moose on the roof?" asks Fletcher.

"Didn't the moose jump off the caboose at the last station?" asks Kristen.

"Well, I can see a moose and a goose," says Fletcher.

"What a mixture," says Kristen.

"A raccoon!" Kristen yells.

"A raccoon?" asks Fletcher. "I see just a moose and a goose."

"Maybe the raccoon is on the roof," says Kristen.

"I am curious," says Fletcher. "Let's check the roof."

"I see gray smoke in the sky," says Kristen. "But not the famous raccoon."

"Wait, I see a skunk," says Fletcher.

"A skunk?" asks Kristen. "Does it have white stripes on its back?"

"No," says Fletcher. "Its fur is black and brown."

Jack just lifted up his head and looked very sad. "Arf! Arf! Arf!" is all he said.

SRA OPEN COURT READING

What Will We Do About Jack?

by Toby Gates
illustrated by Betty Leitzman

Book 37

SRA
A Division of The McGraw-Hill Companies
Columbus, Ohio

www.sra4kids.com
SRA/McGraw-Hill

A Division of The ***McGraw-Hill*** *Companies*

Printed in the United States of America.

Send all inquiries to:
SRA/McGraw-Hill
8787 Orion Place
Columbus, OH 43240-4027

Where is that hound?
Where can he be? Just turn around.

He's not in his doghouse. He's not in the bedroom.
He's not in the bathroom. He's not in the hallway.
He's not in the kitchen. And he's not on the porch.

Where is that hound?
Where can he be? Just turn around.

Jack Did It!

My new kite has a bunch of holes in it.
And I know who did it.

Jack did …
… and then he hid!

My red socks are chewed to tiny bits.
And I know who did it.

Jack did …
… and then
he hid!

Where is that hound?
Where can he be? Just turn around.

Where is that hound?
Where can he be? Just turn around.

Jack did …
… and then he hid!

My backpack has a huge rip in it.
And I know who did it.

Jack did …
… and then he hid!

Where is that hound? Where can he be?
Just turn around.

He's not in his doghouse.
And he's not in the bedroom.

Where is that hound?
Where can he be?
Just turn around.

My homemade cheesecake has a bite out of it.
And I know who did it.

Jack did …
… and then he hid!

Jack did ...
... and then he hid!

Where Is That Hound?

Where is that hound?
Where can he be?
Just turn around.

But the best thing that Fletch and I can do is hug! We hug and hug and hug.

SRA Open Court Reading

Phil and Fletch

by Lisa Trumbauer
illustrated by Guy Porfirio

Book 38

A Division of The McGraw-Hill Companies
Columbus, Ohio

www.sra4kids.com

SRA/McGraw-Hill

A Division of The **McGraw-Hill** *Companies*

Printed in the United States of America.

Send all inquiries to:
SRA/McGraw-Hill
8787 Orion Place
Columbus, OH 43240-4027

Fletch and I can sing.
We sing and sing and sing.

"Stop, Fletch! Please stop, Phil!" says Mom.

Fletch and I can tug!
We tug and help Ranger Claude haul the cat out of the well.

"Go, Fletch! Go, Phil!" says Mom.

Phil and Fletch at Home

I am Phil.
And this is Fletch!
Fletch and I can do lots of things.

Fletch and I can run!
We run and run and run.

"Stop, Fletch! Stop, Phil!
You will wreck the shed!" says Mom.

Fletch and I can spin!
We spin the rope around the tree.
Now they can haul the cat out of the well.

"Go, Fletch! Go, Phil!" says Mom.

Fletch and I can fetch Rangers Paula and Claude!
We fetch the rangers and tell them what we saw.

"Go, Fletch! Go, Phil!" says Mom.

Fletch and I can fetch!
We fetch and fetch and fetch.

"Stop, Fletch! Stop, Phil!
You will wreck the buds!" says Mom.

Fletch and I can spin!
We spin and spin and spin.

"Stop, Fletch! Stop, Phil!
You will wreck that picnic!" says Mom.

Fletch and I can run!
We run and run and run.

"Go, Fletch! Go, Phil!" says Mom.

Phil and Fletch at the Park

I am Phil.
And this is Fletch!
Fletch and I can do lots of things.
Fletch and I can help get your cat!

Fletch and I can tug!
We tug and tug and tug.

"Stop, Fletch! Your jaws will wreck the rug!" says Mom.

Fletch and I can sing.
We sing and sing and sing.
"Pause, Fletch! Please pause, Phil!" says Mom.

"Phil and Fletch, let's go!" says Mom.
"We will go where you can run and fetch.
We will go where you can spin and tug."

"Do you really think I could write my own book?" Bobby asked his dad.

"I know you can. You might even write a very good book," his dad said.

Bobby took the green book from the shelf. "Let's go to the moon."

Books Are No Fun!

by Chloe Texier-Rose
illustrated by Francisco Rodriguez

Book 39

SRA
A Division of The McGraw-Hill Companies
Columbus, Ohio

www.sra4kids.com

SRA/McGraw-Hill

A Division of The **McGraw-Hill** *Companies*

Printed in the United States of America.

Send all inquiries to:
SRA/McGraw-Hill
8787 Orion Place
Columbus, OH 43240-4027

The librarian turned and looked Bobby right in the eyes. "Bobby," she said, "just give books a chance! Who knows? If you read more, then you might write more. If you wrote more, then you might even write your own books! And if you wrote your own books, they would *not* be boring."

Bobby's face lit up.

“Well, you can’t go to the moon. . . except in books.” The librarian pulled down a green book. “I have books with astronauts and animals and heroes and soccer players. I have stories about things that never happened and never will. I have stories of doctors and presidents and knights, too.”

I Just Want to Play

“I don’t want to read any more,” Bobby said. He pushed the book he was reading off his lap.

Dad looked at Bobby with wide eyes. “What’s the matter?” he asked.

"Books are boring, boring, boring!" Bobby cried.

"I don't want to read," he continued. "I want to play outside. I want to talk to my friends. Reading is *so* boring."

"Maybe you just haven't found the right book yet," Dad said.

The librarian was not ready to give up. "We will just have to try something else," she said. She took a different book from the shelf. "This is about Wild Bill. It's set in the Old West."

Bobby said, "No thanks, the Old West doesn't interest me."

The librarian took down a blue book.

"This is a good book," she said.

Bobby opened it up. "This has too many words," he said. He handed the book back to her.

"That's not it," Bobby said. "I think *all* books are boring. I wish I could just play all day."

Dad did not know how to tell Bobby that reading can be fun.

The librarian looked at Bobby. "I think you're wrong about books," she said. "Come with me and I'll show you." She led Bobby to the shelves. "What kind of book would you like to try?" she asked.

"No book," said Bobby.

Bobby said, "Fun is when you laugh and have a good time. Books can't make you have fun!"

Dad had an idea. "Come on, Bobby, let's go."

"Where?" asked Bobby.

"You'll see."

At the Library

The librarian looked up and smiled. "Can I help you?" she asked.

"I have a problem," Dad said. "Bobby here thinks reading is boring."

"Oh, dear," said the librarian. She looked from Dad to Bobby. Bobby just shrugged.

"I am so sorry you feel that way," the librarian said to Bobby. "There are so many books here that are not boring. Some are exciting, and some are full of great and beautiful things. Some are sad, and some are funny."

"Hi, Grandma, are you well?"

"Hi, Grace. I am so glad you came. You are so sweet. My house was too grim and gray and glum to be alone in. But now that you are here with me, I feel glad. Did you bring my stamps and brush? Would you like some lunch? Oh, Grace, I am so glad to see you."

The Gray, Grim House

by Chloe Texier-Rose
illustrated by Francisco Rodriguez

Book 40

SRA
A Division of The McGraw-Hill Companies
Columbus, Ohio

SRA Open Court Reading

www.sra4kids.com

SRA/McGraw-Hill

A Division of The ***McGraw-Hill*** *Companies*

Printed in the United States of America.

Send all inquiries to:
SRA/McGraw-Hill
8787 Orion Place
Columbus, OH 43240-4027

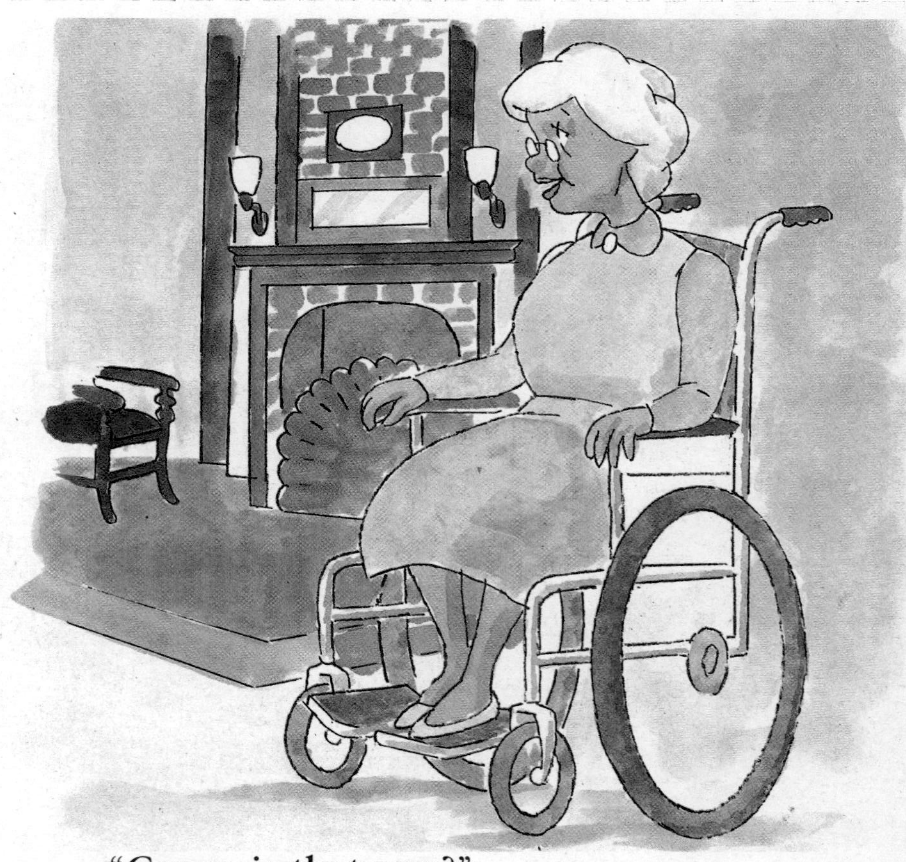

"Grace, is that you?"

Grandma's voice is so sweet. Grace does not know why she felt scared. Sometimes scared just grips and grasps you. Scared can make you glum. But with the help of a sweet voice, scared can melt like sleet and snow.

The dark clouds open up. The sun shines in.

A glint of shiny sun falls on a great, green plant. The great, green plant is mint. It smells so good.

Grace Must Go

"Grace," Mom said.

"Yes, Mom."

"Grace, I need you to go to Grandma's house."

"But, Mom, the rain!"

"Grandma needs you. Take these pants, two plums, some stamps, and Grandma's brush. Don't be scared, Grace. Nothing will harm you."

Gray, gray, gray.
Grim, grim, grim.
Grandma's house is a scary house.
Grace is stuck. Mom trusts her. She must go.

"Grandma? Grandma?"
Now Grace smells a smell.
"Mmmmm! What smells good?"

Grace sees a flash. She hears a smash.
Where is Grandma?

"Grace, take your drum. Bring your snake, Blake. Grandma will be glad to see you both. You can show Grandma how much Blake has grown."

Grace tramps by the train track. High in the sky a small flock of ducks flies over.

The house is dark. Grace hears a drip. Grace hears someone coming. Grace is scared. Grace is glum. In the great, grim house everything is gray.

Grace trips!

“Grandma, Are You Home?”

“Grandma! Grandma! Are you home?” Grace calls. The house is dark. Grace is scared.

“Grandma! Grandma! Are you here?”

Grandma’s house is on a cliff.

Grace sniffs the air. She smells smog. Mist hangs over the land.

Grace passes a truck stuck in the mud. In the back of the truck is a stack of lamps.

Grace hears the rain splash. She stands and stares. She is glad Blake is with her.

The stairs up the cliff are steep. Grace sees Grandma's great, gray, grim house. She climbs the stairs. Blake slips and slogs behind her. Blake likes the rain, but what a trick it is for a snake to climb stairs!

The king spoke to Penrod. "You can keep the ring," he said. "A ring will not make a king."

SRA Open Court Reading

The King's Ring

by Linda Cave
illustrated by Kersti Frigell

Book 41

A Division of The McGraw-Hill Companies
Columbus, Ohio

www.sra4kids.com

SRA/McGraw-Hill

A Division of The ***McGraw-Hill*** *Companies*

Printed in the United States of America.

Send all inquiries to:
SRA/McGraw-Hill
8787 Orion Place
Columbus, OH 43240-4027

"Thank you, my heroes, but I do not need the ruby ring," said the king. "I know that a ring will not make me wise. I need to think. I need to read. That makes me wise."

CHAPTER 1

Once upon a time, there was a wise king. He was nice to those in his kingdom.

The king had a ruby ring. When he wanted to think, he would say, "Bring my ruby ring!" Then he would put on the ring.

CHAPTER 3

The citizens had a plan to rescue the king. They went to the jail and set the real king free. "You are the real king," they said. "Take back the ruby ring!"

He was not wise. He was not fair. He was just mean. The citizens were not happy.

He would think. He would read. He would rub his ring. At last, he would tell the citizens what to do.

The king never lied. He was fair and wise. The citizens truly loved him. But one cruel man did not love him.

Every night Penrod rubbed the jewel. He rubbed and rubbed. He refused to think. He refused to read. The ruby ring did not help him.

Penrod put on the ring. "I am the ruler of the land," said Penrod. So Penrod quickly put the king in jail.

That man was Penrod. Penrod wanted to be king. Penrod had a cruel plan.

CHAPTER 2

After a few days, Penrod hid by the road. He waited for the king. He planned to spring on the king and take his ruby ring.

"Hand over the ruby ring," said Penrod. "The ring will make me wise. Then I will use it to be the king."

"You may take the ring," said the king. "Here it is."

We'd like!

I'd Like

by Chloe Texier-Rose
illustrated by Guy Porfirio

Book 42

SRA
A Division of The McGraw-Hill Companies
Columbus, Ohio

www.sra4kids.com

SRA/McGraw-Hill

A Division of The **McGraw-Hill** *Companies*

Printed in the United States of America.

Send all inquiries to:
SRA/McGraw-Hill
8787 Orion Place
Columbus, OH 43240-4027

"You are right," said Sally Sue. "It is fun to have a friend. To share and share and share. I am glad we are friends. Are you?"

"Yes. It is fun to play together. It is fun to share. It is fun to think about someone besides yourself. It is fun to have a friend, Sally Sue."

I'd Like

I'd like lots of toys in my cart.
I'd like candy bars.
I'd like gum. I'd like cookies. I'd like lots of treats.
I'd like everything in the whole, wide world.

I'd like a kitty. I'd like a puppy that barks.
I'd like a fish. I'd like a pet lark.
I'd like ten cents.

"I am?"

"You are so mean, Sally Sue. You are so selfish. If I had candy, I would share with you. If I had toys, I would play with you. If my mom took me to the park, I would ask if you could come, too. You are my friend."

I'd like to see a movie every day in a row for a whole year.

I'd like to go to the puppet show and sit in the dark.

I'd like to watch TV until my eyes fall out.

I'd like to go to the park.

I'd like to go on a wild sled ride in the snow down a big steep hill.

I'd like to go to a beach with lots of white sand and blue water.

If I want it, no one else can have it.

I don't want anyone else to have anything I'd like. I'd like to be the star. Everything in the whole, wide world will be for me.

I'd like everything in the whole, wide world.
I'd like to be a star.
I'd like to be in my own movie.
I'd like my own band.
I'd like to sing in my own video.

I'd like to go to the zoo.

I'd like my own tiger.

I'd like to go to Mars.

I'd like to jump rope and play double Dutch better than anyone.

Sharing

I'd like everything in the whole, wide world.
I'd like it all just for me.

It is an ear of corn.

SRA Open Court Reading

Silly Riddles

by Doria Romero
illustrated by Karen Tafoya

Book 43

SRA
A Division of The McGraw-Hill Companies
Columbus, Ohio

SRA Open Court Reading

www.sra4kids.com

SRA/McGraw-Hill

A Division of The ***McGraw-Hill*** *Companies*

Printed in the United States of America.

Send all inquiries to:
SRA/McGraw-Hill
8787 Orion Place
Columbus, OH 43240-4027

In order to eat this food you first throw away the outside and cook the inside. Then you eat the outside and throw away the inside.

What is it?

It is an egg.

How Could This Be?

Dawson the rabbit was hungry. Across the lawn, he saw a garden with a fence around it. Dawson's plan was to get into the garden and gnaw at the yummy, raw vegetables. But when he got to the garden, Dawson paused. There was a flaw in his plan. Dawson just fit between the slats of the fence. After he ate, he'd be too fat to get back out. The vegetables were too big to fit through the slats.

Dawson ate as many vegetables as he wanted without getting stuck in the garden.

How could this be?

Dawson crawled into the garden. Then he hauled the vegetables to the edge of the fence. He left them on the inside and squeezed back out. Then he sat down and ate the vegetables through the fence.

This is something that must always be broken before it is used.

What is it?

It is a quarter in Paula's pocket.

Officer Law went for a walk. While he was out, it started to rain. He did not have an umbrella or a rain hat with him. His uniform was soaked, but not a hair on his head got wet.

How could this be?

Officer Law's hair didn't get wet because he is bald.

What Is It?

Paula the astronaut was camping in August. One morning at dawn, she woke up, stretched, and yawned. Then she felt something in her pocket. It had a head and a tail, but it had no legs. Paula found no cause for alarm.

What is it?

Rosa didn't need the light because she was reading Braille.

Five girls walked to school under one tiny umbrella. Not one of the girls got wet.

How could this be?

The girls stayed dry because it wasn't raining.

One night, Rosa was sitting in her chair, reading a book. Because she felt chilly, she got up to get a shawl. Suddenly, there was a blackout—all the lights went out. Rosa had no flashlights or candles, but she wrapped the shawl around her and kept on reading.

How could this be?

"There it is!" said Mike. "I knew you wouldn't forget!"

When Uncle Mooney looked, he saw that the blue tie was right there on his neck. He looked back up at Mike and smiled.

"Here," he said, handing Mike the tray, "have a root beer and a few macaroons."

SRA Open Court Reading

The Blue Tie

by Ellen Garin
illustrated by Kersti Frigell

Book 44

SRA
A Division of The McGraw-Hill Companies
Columbus, Ohio

www.sra4kids.com

SRA/McGraw-Hill

A Division of The **McGraw-Hill** *Companies*

Printed in the United States of America.

Send all inquiries to:
SRA/McGraw-Hill
8787 Orion Place
Columbus, OH 43240-4027

Uncle Mooney's face got red and hot. "Well," he said to Mike as he unbuttoned his sweater, "you see. . . I. . . um. . . ."

There was nothing left to do. Uncle Mooney simply had to tell Mike the bad news. He went to the living room and placed the tray of food on the table.

"Wait!" said Mike. "Uncle Mooney, where's the blue tie? We can't see a game without the lucky blue tie."

Where Is That Tie?

One Tuesday in June, Uncle Mooney was hunting for his blue tie. First, he tried the closet, but the tie wasn't there. Then he tried his dresser, but the tie wasn't there. He even tried underneath the bed, but the blue tie was still missing.

This was a huge problem for Uncle Mooney. The tie was a gift from his nephew, Mike. Every Tuesday afternoon, Mike came over to see the game on TV. Uncle Mooney wore the blue tie. It was good luck.

Mike went into the living room and turned on the TV. Uncle Mooney went to the kitchen and fixed a tray of snack foods.

"Hurry up, Uncle Mooney. You are going to miss the first pitch," yelled Mike.

Uncle Mooney was not in a good mood. He didn't like to hurt Mike's feelings. When Mike knocked, Uncle Mooney gloomily opened the door.

"I'm sorry I'm late," said Mike. "We had better hurry. The game will be on soon."

"Hmmm. Last week I spilled root beer on the tie. Maybe Mike took it to be cleaned," said Uncle Mooney to himself. "Mike likes to do nice things like that."

"I know," said Uncle Mooney, "I'll ask Mike's sister, Sue. Maybe she knows. I just hope that Sue picks up the phone. I'd rather not tell Mike that I lost the lucky tie just yet."

Uncle Mooney phoned Mike's house. Sue picked up right away.

"Whew!" said Uncle Mooney. "I'm glad it's you. Do you know whether Mike took my blue tie to be cleaned?"

Time to Tell the Truth

Late in the afternoon, Uncle Mooney woke up.

"Oh, no!" he said. "Mike will be here soon. It is too late to do anything about it. I will just have to tell him that I lost the lucky tie."

He was so tired from his hunt that he decided to sit for a bit. Soon, he was napping.

"No, he didn't," said Sue. "Mike had to take things to the cleaner for Mom, and he didn't have the blue tie when he went."

"Thanks, Sue," said Uncle Mooney. "I hope to see you soon," he added.

"It must be here somewhere," Uncle Mooney muttered to himself. He tried every room in his house. He went into the attic and under the roof beams. He glanced inside his huge tuba. He even looked in his new boots. But there was still no lucky blue tie.

Uncle Mooney began to brood. "Where is that tie?" he asked himself.